MEMOIRS
OF
HENRY OBOOKIAH

MEMOIRS

OF

HENRY OBOOKIAH,

A NATIVE OF OWHYHEE,

AND A MEMBER OF THE

FOREIGN MISSION SCHOOL;

WHO DIED AT

CORNWALL, CONNECTICUT FEBRUARY 17, 1818,

AGED 26 YEARS.

By EDWIN W. DWIGHT

WOMAN'S BOARD OF MISSIONS

FOR THE PACIFIC ISLANDS

HONOLULU, HAWAI'I

Manufactured in the United States of America

ISBN: 0615650333
ISBN-13: 978-0615650333

Cover and Frontispiece: The engraving of Henry Obookiah used on the cover and for the frontispiece was first used in the 1818 and 1819 editions of the **Memoirs.** The original 1818 copper engraving plate is in the collection of the Cornwall Historical Society, Cornwall, Connecticut.

Distributed by
Woman's Board of Missions for the Pacific Islands
1848 Nuʻuanu Avenue
Honolulu, Hawaiʻi 96817

Design and manufacture of this book was through the services of

The Larry Czerwonka Company
Hilo, Hawaii

"He came to this land,
and heard of Him
on whom without hearing, he could not
believe,
and by the mouth of those, who could never
have spoken to him
in Owhyhee."
---Rev. Lyman Beecher
February 18, 1818

These lines are quoted from the Funeral Oration given by the Rev. Dr. Lyman Beecher at the meeting house in Cornwall, Connecticut, on February 18, 1818. Beecher, famous for his revivalist preaching, occupied the pulpit at nearby Litchfield, Connecticut, at the time of Obookiah's death. The entire oration was bound with the 1818 and 1819 editions of the *Memoirs of Henry Obookiah*.

CONTENTS

Contents

Photo section precedes page 1

EDITOR'S PREFACE
TO THE 1968 EDITION

IN THE little village of Cornwall, set in the Litchfield Hills, the northwest corner of Connecticut, there is a country graveyard. Walk up the steep bank, past the old headstones tilted in the tall grass, or, depending on the season, the deep snow, and you will come to a large, flat stone resting on a quadrangular tomb of rocks. The inscription, worn and weathered by a thousand New England storms, is still easy to read.

IN
Memory of
HENRY OBOOKIAH
a native of
OWHYHEE.
His arrival in this country gave rise
to the Foreign mission school,
of which he was a worthy member.
He was once an Idolater, and was
designed for a Pagan Priest; but by
the grace of God and by the prayers
and instructions of pious friends,
he became a Christian.
He was eminent for piety and
missionary Zeal. When almost prepared
to return to his native Isle to preach the
Gospel. God took to himself. In his last
sickness, he wept and prayed for Owhyhee,
but was submissive. He died without fear
with a heavenly smile on his
countenance and glory in his soul.
Feb. 17, 1818;
Aged 26

Who was this "Henry Obookiah" and what is he doing here in this Yankee cemetery? What brought him so far from his native place to lie in this corner of a foreign field? What is the story behind this tombstone?

This book, *Memoirs of Henry Obookiah,* tells that story—and a remarkable, touching, human story it is. It begins on an island in the middle of the warm Pacific and ends in the cold, cold ground of Connecticut. It starts with a bloody battle between two tribes and finished, not many years later, with a quiet death in a country parsonage.

It is a tale of two cultures—Hawaiian and New England. It is the story of *Aloha* in a land which had not the word but had at least the spirit; the story of an island boy who never made it back to the islands—but whose life and death helped to make the islands what they are today.

Take a long look at that gravestone: it is the hinge on which the door of the history of modern Hawaii swung.

—Edith Wolfe

Honolulu, Hawaii
October I, 1967 A.D.

ACKNOWLEDGEMENTS

The Woman's Board of Missions for the Pacific Islands is grateful to hold the copyright to the *Memoirs of Henry Obookiah*. We have been entrusted with a blessed gift of great historical value. We cannot forget our predecessors who have gone before us. The Reverend Edith Wolfe capably edited the 1968 edition. It was the 150th Anniversary of the original printing that had once inspired many living on the East Coast to give up their lifestyle and move to Hawai'i to spread the gospel of Jesus Christ.

Many organizations, including the United Church Board for World Ministries Library, the Houghton Library of Harvard University, Andover Newton Theological School, the Archives of Hawai'i, the Hawaiian Historical Society, the Connecticut Conference of the United Church of Christ, Yale University, the Yale University Library, the Litchfield North Association, the Congregational Churches in Cornwall, Litchfield, Norfolk, Goshen and Torringford, the Congregational Church in Hollis, New Hampshire, the Christian Historical Society, and the Connecticut Historical Society provided vital assistance when called upon more than 50 years ago, and this book stands as a testament to their faithfulness.

A kindhearted appreciation is also felt for the Library of the Union Theological Seminary, the American Bible Society, the American Tract Society, the U.S. Department of the Interior, the Library of the American Congregational Association, and the Congregational Christian Historical Society for past services.

Individual thanks for the vintage pictures in the book go to Catherine Williams, Virginia Dupouy, and Pat Swenson. We also commend Mary Jane Knight and Daphne Yamamoto for locating many of the older photos used in the 1990 and 2012 editions of this book.

We extend our warmest mahalo to Margaret S. Ehlke, editor of the 1990 edition. She provided the research and revisions of chapters and photo notes, an expanded index, and helpful suggestions concerning the book format, which will also be used in the 2012 edition.

The WBMPI is also thrilled to bring the new in with the old, and it is a great honor to present the "rest of the story" in the form of a brand new epilogue pertaining to Henry Opukaha'ia's final journey back to the Big Island of Hawai'i. We appreciate the many hours and days Deborah Lee selflessly gave to provide an in-depth first person account of the activity surrounding his return home, as well as the additional time required to edit and revise the story.

The WBMPI imparts a special thank you to the Reverend Alan Tamashiro of Hilo, Hawai'i, for donating pictures of Henry 'Opukaha`ia's former gravesite in Cornwall, Connecticut, and to our current president, Karen Welsh, for traveling to Kepulu, Hawai'i to take pictures of his new resting place at Kahikolu Congregational Church Cemetery, overlooking the cliffs of Kealakekua Bay for the 2012 edition.

We would also like to thank each of our members who have faithfully prayed the current printing to its full conclusion. We appreciate our WBMPI Interim Executive Director Clara D. Priester for her enthusiasm and support and we particularly thank one special angel amongst our membership who provided the funding for this project, as we could not have proceeded without her generosity.

We thank the The Reverend Dr. Charles A. Buck and the Hawai`i Conference of the United Church of Christ for their unfailing encouragement for this project.

Most of all, we would like to thank Jesus Christ, from Whom all blessings flow. It is through His continued grace and mercy that the Woman's Board of Missions for the Pacific Islands has been able to maintain a clear vision and a mission to tell others about the good news that comes through salvation. We have faithfully served Hawai`i and the Pacific Rim for more than 140 years, and by His will, we will continue throughout the next millennium.

INTRODUCTION

SOMEWHAT MORE than a century and a half ago, a fifteen-year-old boy looked out across Kealakekua Bay on the west coast of the island called Hawaii and wondered about the handsome square-rigger he saw anchored there. He had watched many another sailing ship enter and leave the bay, and always he has said to himself, "Where has it come from?"

"Where will it go?" "Will it ever come again?" On this day he added the thought" "Why don't I try to find out?"

It was, as he put it later, only "a boy's notion," but it led him, first to the cabin of the *Triumph*, where he talked with the captain, and afterwards to China, New York City, to New Haven and, eventually, to Cornwall, Connecticut.

In Cornwall, on February 17, 1818, half a world away from home, he died at the age of twenty-six.

That should have been the end of his story. But it was not.

A few months after his death a book appeared in New England—a thin, brown-covered volume of a hundred small pages. It told, in his own words and the words of those who had known him the story of the boy's life and death. The printer who set the type, struck off the sheets and bound them together did not know it, but that book was to launch a ship and a movement that was to transform Hawaii. For the boy was Opukaha'ia (his American friends spelled and pronounced it *Obookiah*), and his life and early death and his hope of taking Christianity to his people were the inspiration for the Sandwich Islands Mission. The ship launched was the *Thaddeus*, which sailed with the pioneer company from Boston in October, 1819. In the long run, the American Board of Commissioners for Foreign Missions sent eighty-four men and one hundred women to Hawaii to preach and teach, to translate and publish, to advise, and counsel—and win the hearts of the Hawaiian people.

In this memoir, today's reader will find a young man in his late teens and early twenties, in some ways totally different from his mid-Twentieth Century counterparts, but basically much like them. Unhappy with his lot, brooding almost to the point of suicide over the cruel events that had robbed him of his family, dissatisfied with the career his elders had chosen for him and the rigid course of training he must undergo to prepare for it, Opukaha'ia recognized them. Tradition says he wept as he sat on the steps of Yale's main building, If there were tears in his eyes as he sat there, it was because he saw, crossing the campus, young men who carried books. Locked in those books, he knew, was wisdom far beyond what his priest-uncle had taught him at Napoopoo. When a way was opened for him to learn to read, he seized it. As to friendships, he valued them highly, He was fortunate in the people he met—on shipboard and in a dozen New England communities—and there was something in his countenance and his character that drew people to him, and made them want to help him.

Opukaha'ia, the Hawaiian priest's apprentice, was deliberate and thoughtful in his consideration of the doctrines of Christianity, but, in the end, he accepted the new religion with his whole heart. He, who had mourned for his family, found that he had a Father in heaven and brothers throughout the earth. He, who had been a restless wanderer, found that he had as much dignity and worth as any king or chief. He whose life had been aimless found a purpose.

The *Memoirs* reveal him as happy in New England, even when the weather was harsh and the snows deep, but as thinking ever of his homeland, where he would one day twit the priests about their futile wooden gods, gain the King's permission to set up schools, and proclaim the gospel as he had received it. What a missionary Opukaha'ia would have made if he had lived to finish his studies and sail back to Hawaii!

But it was not to be. As Lyman Beecher said in his sermon preached at the funeral service for Opukaha'ia: *"We thought surely this is he who shall comfort Owhyhee...We bury with his dust in the grave all our high raised hopes of his future activity in the cause of Christ."*

There in the grave it might have ended. But then came the book.

Because they felt his vibrant presence in the *Memoirs*, men and women who never knew Opukaha'ia in the flesh volunteered to carry his message after his death. In fact, of the fourteen Americans who sailed in the *Thaddeus*, only Samuel Ruggles had ever met Opukaha'ia face to face. Hiram Bingham visited the Foreign Mission School in Cornwall, but that wasn't until the spring of 1819, when Opukaha'ia had been dead a year. Daniel Chamberlain enrolled his two oldest sons in the school for a term, but that was only after the Obookiah of the *Memoirs* had moved him and his wife to offer themselves as missionaries. It was the talk that the book stirred among Yale undergraduates that made Samuel Whitney, a sophomore, decide to forego further study and apply at once for a place in the mission company. Elisha Loomis, printer's apprentice in the frontier town of Canandaigua, New York, would never have heard of Opukaha'ia—indeed, might scarcely have discovered the difference between Honolulu and Hong Kong—if he had not chanced upon a copy of the *Memoirs.*

Among the church people of its day the book was a best seller. Men read it and sent generous gifts to the American Board to help finance a mission to the Sandwich Islands. Women read it and let it be known that they would go gladly to the Pacific if only young missionaries who needed "companions" would look their way. Little girls read it and "abstained from sugar" in order to save fifty cents to donate to the cause.

Slender and simple as it was, this book shaped the future of Hawaii.

There are those, of course, who say it would have been better if the book had not been written—if the missionaries had never come. Then, so the argument runs, Hawai'i might have remained an "unspoiled paradise" of picturesque wooden images, feather capes, outrigger canoes and poetic hulas. But persons who argue thus are forgetting Captain Cook.

Look again at Kealakekua Bay. Over on the northern shore, clearly visible from Napoopoo, stands the monument that marks the place of Cook's death. Only three decades before Opukaha'ia swam out to the *Triumph,* Cook's ships—*Discovery* and *Resolution*—had lain off shore there. After Cook, the world came—at first slowly, then with increasing rapidity—adventures, refugees, traders, whalers, merchants, and eventually, tourists.

Who can guess what Hawai'i would be like today if only these others had come and the missionaries had not? No one can be sure, but this much we can say with certainty: when a country opens its doors to outsiders and seeks a place among the nations of the world, it is fortunate if some of the newcomers bring education, democracy and a gospel of brotherhood.

If, then, at Kealakekua, we ponder the life of Captain James Cook, which ended here, we must likewise give grateful thought to Opukaha'ia, whose voyage began here. Though he knew not what he sought when he left home, he prized the treasure when he found it and with his dying breath asked that it be bestowed upon Hawai'i.

—Albertine Loomis

KA MOOLELO

o

HENERI OPUKAHAIA,

UA HANAUIA MA HAWAII, M. H. 1787,

A

UA MAKE MA AMERIKA,

FEBERUARI 17, 1818.

OIA KA HUA MUA O HAWAII NEI.

PAIIA E

KO AMERIKA AHAHUI TERAKA,

NU IOKA.

1867.

The Title Page of the Hawaiian edition of the "Memoirs" published in 1867 by the American Tract Society for the Hawaiian Sunday Schools. Translator Rev. S. W. Papaula, minister at the Kahikolu Church in Kealakekua, Hawai'i, interviewed people at Napo'opo'o for information on Opukaha'ia's (the later Hawaiian spelling) family. (Courtesy HMCS Library)

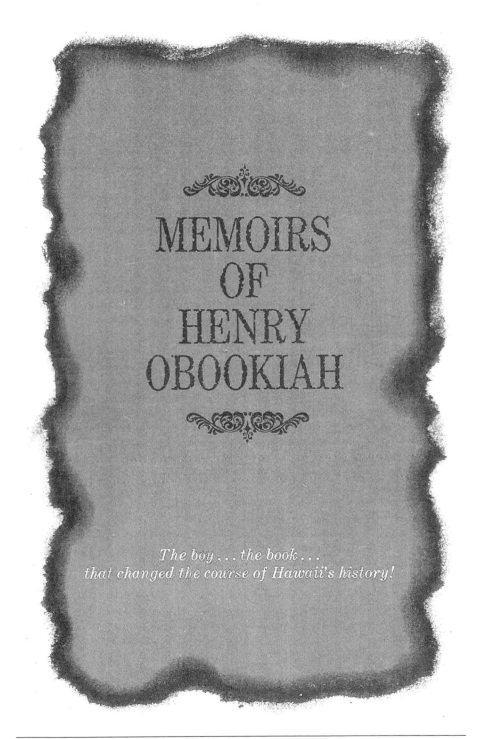

MEMOIRS

OF

HENRY

OBOOKIAH

The boy . . . the book . . .
that changed the course of Hawaii's history!

The Title Page of the "Memoirs" published in 1968 by the Woman's Board of Missions for the Pacific Islands to honor the "150th Anniversary of His Death." Cover design by Charles Taketa.

150th ANNIVERSARY EDITION

MEMOIRS OF HENRY OBOOKIAH

"IT IS GOOD NEWS, indeed, that the MEMOIRS OF HENRY OBOOKIAH is again available in print. Those who for many years have longed to lay their hands on a copy will rejoice. It is to be hoped that unnumbered others who may never have heard of it will take advantage of the opportunity to make the acquaintance of one of the most unusual and remarkable Christians of the nineteenth century, and of the book, certainly one of the most influential of that century, which recounts his all too brief life story . . . Here is a tale unsurpassed in romance, poignancy and enduring effect."

— Henry Pitney Van Dusen
President Emeritus
Union Theological Seminary, New York

In the year 1809, a young Hawaiian orphan leaped into Kealakekua Bay and swam out to a sailing vessel anchored in the harbor. That leap carried Henry Obookiah (Opukahaia) from pagan Hawaii to Puritan New England. There, for ten years, in a land so distant and so different from his own, the island boy found a new life, a new faith and a hope for "Owhyhee" that he did not live to see fulfilled. So impressed were the New Englanders by this remarkable young man, that within a year following his death in 1818 at the age of 26, they launched a ship from Boston that carried the beginnings of the modern world to the Sandwich Islands. Henry Obookiah's was the face that launched that ship. Thousands of ships and planes have followed that one.

Edited by EDITH WOLFE

Introduction by ALBERTINE LOOMIS

The Back Cover of the "Memoirs" published in 1968 by the Woman's Board of Missions for the Pacific Islands. Design by Charles Taketa

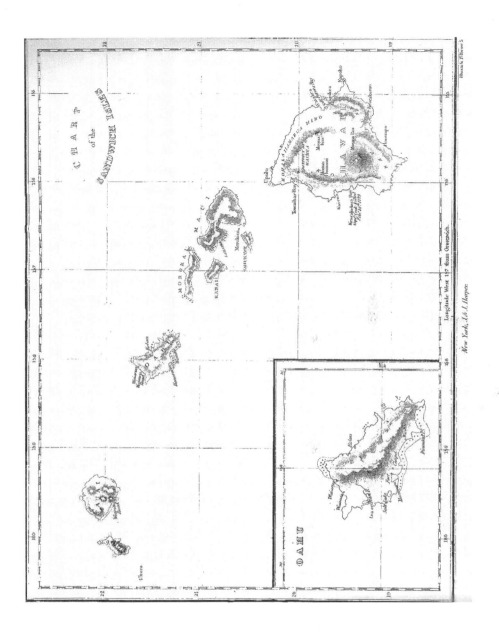

Chart of the Sandwich Isles. This was included in the 1833 edition of *Polynesian Researches During a Residence of Nearly Eight Years in the Society and Sandwich Islands* by William Ellis (Volume IV), and the *"Memoirs"* published in 1968. On this chart the confusion which existed between the use of the "k" and "t," the "r" and "l" are clearly shown. (Cf. *"Tauai" which is now "Kauai," "Morokai" which is now "Molokai," "Waititi" which is now "Waikiki."*)

Kealakekua Bay on the island of Hawai'i from a drawing by John Webber of the Cook Expedition in 1779. The Hikiau Heaiu at Napo'opo'o, in the right foreground, was home to Opukaha'ia as he trained to become a pagan priest. The Ship *Triumph,* Caleb Brintnall, master, anchored here in 1808 and Opukaha'ia began his journey to New England. (Courtesy HMCS Library)

Friendly Priest's House, Napo'opo'o, Hawai'i, depicts the home of a priest at the Hikiau Heiau, at the time of Cook's Expedition in 1779. Opukaha'ia's uncle, Pahoa, was a celebrated priest at Hikiau who had been instructed by Heehawed, the high priest of the temple, according to Hawaiian historian Charles W. Kenn. (From a watercolor artist William W. Ellis, courtesy the Bernice P. Bishop Museum.)

Hikiau Heiau at Napo'opo'o, on the shore of Kealakekua Bay, as it looked in 1890. Captain James Cook was honored as the Hawaiian god Lono in ceremonies at this heiau in January 1779. (Courtesy the Bernice P. Bishop Museum.)

The Four Owhyean Youths print was sold to benefit the Sandwich Islands Missions in 1822. Obookiah's friends and fellow students at the Foreign Mission School, Thomas Hopu, who had sailed with him on the Ship *Triumph,* William Kanui, John Honoli'i, and George Kaumuali'i, returned to Hawai'i with the Pioneer Company of Sandwich Islands missionaries aboard the Brig *Thaddeus* in 1820. (Courtesy HMCS Library)

An Owhihe Grammar.

The parts of speech, as in most other languages, are nine: the Article, Noun, Pronoun, Adjective, Verb, Adverb, Conjunction, Preposition, and Interjection.

The Article.

The articles are four, O, Ohs, Ohe and Ha.

The article O is placed before the personal pronouns, and also before the names of persons and places; as O-ou, I — O e, Thou — O-o-3-ls, He, She or It. O-whi-he   O-mon-3-has &c.

The article O is declined in the following manner:

N. O.
P. O-ha.
O. E-3.

The articles Ohs and Ohe are placed before all nouns, except the names of persons and places, and are declined thus:

N. Ohs	N. Ohe
P. Oho	P. Oho
O. Ehs	O. Ehe

A Short Elementary Grammar of the Owhihe Language is in the collection of the Hawaiian Historical Society, Honolulu. The Grammar is credited to Obookiah. Evidently he had assistance from the Rev. Eleazer T. Fitch of Yale College as he wrote to Fitch, June 14, 1815. "I want to see you about our Grammar: I want to get through with it." (Courtesy the Hawaiian Historical Society)

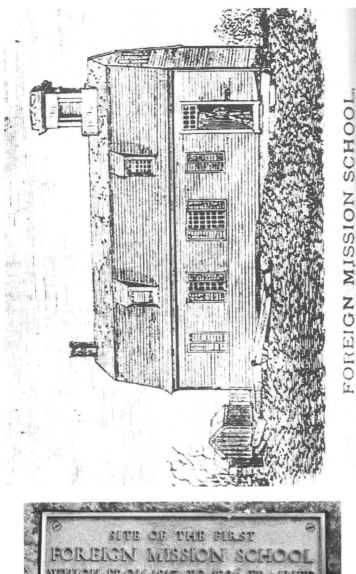

FOREIGN MISSION SCHOOL.

The Foreign Mission School in Cornwall, Connecticut, began its operations in 1817, educating students of many races to become missionaries to their own peoples during the almost 10 years of its existence. Edwin W. Dwight was the first instructor, serving until May 1817 when the Rev. Herman Daggett became principal of the institution. (Courtesy HMCS Library) Second photo of the plaque commemorating the school is by Alan Tamashiro.

The Reverend Dr. Timothy Dwight, President of Yale College, gave Obookiah a home for several months after his arrival in New Haven. Dwight was one of the Agents appointed by the ABCFM "to establish and conduct a school for the education of heathen youth." Meeting at Dwight's home in 1816, they adopted a Constitution for the Foreign Mission School. (Portrait in Yale University Art Gallery, gift of individuals of the class of 1817. John Turnbull, painter.)

The Grave of Henry Obookiah sat on a hillside in the Cornwall, Connecticut, cemetery before his remains were removed by family and taken back to Napo'opo'o, on the shore of Kealakekua Bay in 1993. The flat marble tombstone that still marks Obookiah's grave was placed there though private subscription at a cost of $28. (J. P. M. Swenson Photo)

The Inscription on the former Tombstone of Henry Obookiah tells the story of the Hawaiian youth who had been expected to bring Christianity to Hawai'i. (Courtesy HMCS Library)

The former gravesite of Henry Obookiah as it stands in 2010. (Alan Tamashiro Photo)

The House in which Henry Obookiah Died was the parsonage of the Rev. Timothy Stone, minister at the Cornwall Church in 1818. It is still used as a residence in Cornwall. (C. H. W. Photo)

The Room in which Obookiah Died as it looked in 1968. (J. P. M. Swenson Photo)

uch affection — The day Henery died he had great enjoyment in God and a heavenly smile appeared on his countenance through the day & continued till after death — He shook hands with them & bade them farewell a few minuets before his death saying he was not afraid to die and died without a struggle — Miss Stone attended upon him constantly during his sickness — She appears to be raised above the world — said the day of his death was the happiest one she ever knew & it was her earnest wish to die like him and should be the business of her life to prepare to meet him in heaven — Henery had a desire to recover that he might preach the gospel to his countrymen — He sent a note to the meetinghouse on the sabbath requesting prayers that his life might be preserved & he permitted to return & preach the gospel to his countrymen but whether he lived or died God might be glorified — One of the last things he said was I shall never go to Owhyhee After the exercises at the meeting house were over they proceeded to the burying ground — The corpse was set down & the singing immediately began in a solem manner this anthem — And I heard a voice from heaven saying unto me write from henceforth, Blessed are the dead &c — the effect you can conceive better than I can tell you After this Mr Dwight made a few remarks — Said that in the glorious death of the dear young man whom they then committed to the dust all who had interested & exerted themselves for his instruction had a rich reward — It would alone be a rich reward for all that had been would be done for these youths — He said he came to this country to teach christians how to die — & Mr Dwight appeared deeply afflicted

---

The Letter from Miss Daggett, February 27, 1818, describes the funeral services for Henry Obookiah and the ceremonies at graveside in Cornwall Cemetery on February 18, 1818. (Courtesy the Connecticut Historical Society, Hartford, Connecticut)

Inscription on the Opukaha'ia Monument at Napo'opo'o, Hawai'i, is written in both English and Hawaiian. It was first erected at the foot of Hikiau Heiau in 1920 to honor the Hawaiian youth on the 100th anniversary of the arrival of the American Protestant Mission to Hawai'i and then moved near Henry's final resting place at Kahikolu Church in Napo'opo'o, overlooking Kealakekua Bay. (Karen Welsh Photo)

do not forget to write to as soon as when ev
you could I wish could write plainer tha
what I have now; please to present my
humble respects to all of your friends an
Mr. Ripley and all family; I subscribe you
sincerely and afflectionate Friend

Mrs. Florella M. Ripley   Henry Obookiah

I have not heard any news except those
missionaries are going to Asaia, vz.
Horta Bradwell, Benjamin C. Meigs
Daniel Poor,   ...   me Richards

Obookiah's Letter to Mrs. Florilla (Mills) Ripley illustrates the mastery of penmanship and the English language. Mrs. Ripley was a sister of Samuel J. Mills, Jr., and lived in Cornish, New Hampshire. The letter had been hand delivered by Obookiah to her father, according to a postscript by Father Mills. (Courtesy HMCS Library)

The Opukaha'ia Memorial Chapel and the *Plaque at the Chapel* at Punalu'u, Ka'u. Hawai'i commemorates the life of the young man who "inspired the first American Board Mission to Hawaii." Opukaha'ia was born in the district of Ka'u. The Chapel was completed in 1957 by the Laymen's Fellowship with gifts from the Woman's Board of Missions and the Congregational Christian churches of Hawai'i. (Karen Welsh Photos)

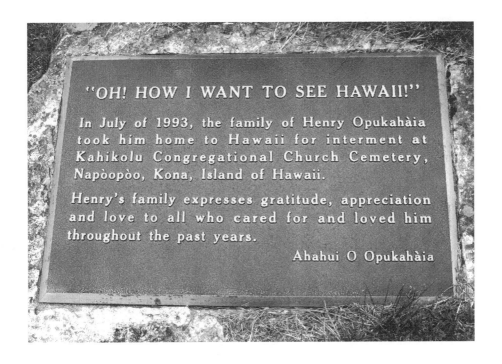

"OH! HOW I WANT TO SEE HAWAII!"

In July of 1993, the family of Henry Opukahàia took him home to Hawaii for interment at Kahikolu Congregational Church Cemetery, Napòopòo, Kona, Island of Hawaii.

Henry's family expresses gratitude, appreciation and love to all who cared for and loved him throughout the past years.

Ahahui O Opukahàia

The plaque placed by the AHAHUI O `OPUKAHA`IA (Friends and family joined in the effort to bring his body home) on the former gravesite of Henry Obookiah to signify the importance of his life and conversion to Christianity in Connecticut. (Alan Tamashiro Photo)

The historic Hawaiian Kahikolu Church at Napo'opo'o, on the hillside overlooking Kealakekua Bay, is the site of Henry O`pukaha`ia's final resting place. He was brought back to the islands in 1993 by loving family and friends. (Karen Welsh photo)

Pictured in 2003: Kahu (Pastor) Wendell Davis of Kahikolu Church, on the far right, with the Lee family, all descendants of the Opukaha'ia ohana. They had gathered together for a special commemoration of the 10-year anniversary of the dedication of his gravesite. Deborah Li'ikapeka Lee, second from the right, assisted with the exhumation of Opukaha'ia's remains from Cornwall, Connecticut to the Big Island of Hawai'i in 1993. (C.E. Chambers Photo)

Deborah Li`ikapeka Lee heard God's voice calling her to bring back the body of her family member in 1992. Nine months later she succeeded. She is pictured here in 2012 at his new resting place overlooking Kealakekua Bay. (Karen Welsh Photo)

A picture of Henry Opukaha'ia, draped with Maile lei, inside of Kahikolu Church at Napo'opo'o, on the hillside overlooking Kealakekua Bay. (Karen Welsh Photo)

CHAPTER I

HISTORY
BEFORE REACHING AMERICA

HENRY OBOOKIAH was a native of Hawaii, the most important and populous of the Sandwich Islands. He was born about the year 1792. His parents ranked with the common people, but his mother was related to the family of the king. Her name was Kummo'o'olah.

The name of his father is unknown. When Obookiah was at the age of ten or twelve, both his parents were slain before his eyes, "in a war," to use his own language, "made after the old king died, to see who should be great among them." The only surviving member of the family, beside himself, was an infant brother two or three months old. This little brother he hoped to save from the destruction that befell his parents, and took him upon his back to flee from the enemy; but was overtaken, and the child cruelly destroyed. The circumstances of this interesting scene are described in a "Narrative of Heathen Youth," by Rev. Joseph Harvey, as taken from the relation of Obookiah.

"Two parties were contending for the dominion of the island. The warriors met and a dreadful slaughter ensued. The party to which the father of Obookiah belonged was overpowered. The conquerors, having driven their antagonists from the field, next turned their rage upon the villages and families of the vanquished. The alarm was given of their approach. The father, taking his wife and two children, fled to the mountains. There he concealed himself for several days with his family in a cave. But, at length, being driven by thirst to leave their retreat, they went in quest of water to a neighboring spring. Here they were surprised by a party of the enemy while in the act of quenching their thirst. The father, obeying the first impulse of nature, fled, but the cries of his wife and children soon brought him back again for their protection. But seeing the enemy near, again he fled. The enemy seeing the affection of the father for his family, having seized his wife and children, put them to torture, in order to decoy him from his retreat. The artifice succeeded. Unable to bear the piercing cries of his family, again he appeared, and fell into their hands, and, with his wife, was cut in pieces. While this was going on, Obookiah being then a lad of about twelve years, took his infant brother upon his back and attempted to make his escape. But he was pursued, and his little brother pierced through with a Pahooa, or spear, while on his back. He himself was saved alive, because he was not young enough to give them trouble, nor old enough to excite their fears."

Obookiah now being a prisoner in the hands of the enemy, was taken home to the house of the very man who murdered his parents. With him he remained until he was found by an uncle, who having obtained the consent of his keeper, took him into his own family and treated him as his child. This uncle was a priest, and had the rank of high priest of the island. It was his design to educate Obookiah for the same service. In pursuance of this purpose, he taught him long prayers, and trained him to the task of repeating them daily in the temple of the idol. This ceremony he sometimes commenced before sunrise in the morning, and at other times was employed in it during the whole or the greater part of the night. Parts of these prayers he often repeated to gratify the curiosity of his friends, after he came to this country. They regarded the weather, the general prosperity of the island, its defense from enemies, and especially the life and happiness of the king.

He continued with his uncle, and in this employment, until he took his departure from his native country, to go in quest of another, where he hoped to find the happiness which the death of his parents had taken from him, and which nothing now to be found in his own country could supply.

His feelings on this subject, with some account of his situation while he remained upon the island, of his departure for America, and his reception in this country, are found in a history of his past life written by himself several years before his death. As this, to all the readers of these memoirs, will doubtless be interesting, considered as the production of a heathen youth, the greater part of it will be inserted, with but few slight alterations. His own ideas, and, in general, his own language will be preserved. The history commences at the time of his parents' death.

"The same man," says he, "which killed my father and mother took me home to his own house. His wife was an amiable woman, and very kind, and her husband also; yet, on account of his killing my parents, I did not feel contented. After I lived with this man about a year or two, I found one of my uncles, who was a priest among them; but he knew not what I was—(for I was quite small when he saw me at home with my parents.) He inquired the name of my parents—I told him. As soon as he heard the name of my parents, tears burst out and he wept bitterly. He wished me not to go back and live with that man which killed my father and mother, but live with him as long as I live. I told him I must go back and see that man whether he was willing to give me a release. This was done. I went home and told the man all what my uncle had told me. But the saying seemed to him very unpleasing. As soon as he heard all what I said to him, he was very tormented with anger, as if he would look me in pieces that moment. He would not let me go, not till he die, or else he take my life away. Not long after this I went and told my uncle what the man had told me, and he would no more let me go back to the man's house, until the man come after me, then he would converse with him on this subject. After I had lived with my uncle two or three days, the man came to his house to take me home. But my uncle told him that I was as his own child—that he would not let me go back and live with him; else if he take me, he should take both of us. Yet the man did say but little, because my uncle was a priest. But he told my uncle that if I should live with him, he must take kind care of me, as he himself had done. He told him he would by all means. When all this was done, I lived with my uncle a number of years."

It was probably during this period, and before peace was entirely restored to the Island that an event occurred in which the hand of Providence was strikingly visible in rescuing Obookiah from a second exposure to a violent and untimely death. Let the reader mark the goodness of God, and the kind designs, as in the case of Joseph, which he had to accomplish in behalf of Henry's kindred and countrymen, as well as himself, in sparing his life. He, with an aunt, the only surviving sister of his father, had fallen into the hands of the enemy. On a certain day it came to his knowledge that his aunt, and perhaps himself, was to be put to death. The first opportunity he could find he attempted to make his escape. And by creeping through a hole into a cellar, and going out on the opposite side, he got away unobserved, and wandered off at a considerable distance from the house in which he had been kept. But it was not long before his aunt was brought out by a number of the enemy, and taken to a precipice from which she was thrown and destroyed. He saw this—and now feeling himself more than ever alone, as soon as the enemy had retired he ran toward the fatal spot, resolved to throw himself over and die with this friend, whom perhaps he now considered as the last individual of his kindred. But he was discovered by one of the chiefs or head-men of the party, who ordered two men to pursue him and bring him back. He was overtaken just before he reached the precipice, carried back to the quarters of the enemy, and mercifully saved for purposes which will appear in the subsequent history.

"At the death of my parents," he says, "I was with them; I saw them killed with a bayonet—and with them my little brother, not more than two or three months old. So that I was left alone without father and mother in this wilderness world. Poor boy, thought I within myself, after they were gone, are there any father or mother of mine at home, that I may go find them at home? No, poor boy am I. And while I was at play with other children—after we had made an end of playing, they return to their parents—but I was returned into tears; —for I have no home, neither father nor mother. I was now brought away from my home to a strange place, and I thought of nothing more but want of father and mother, and to cry day and night.

"While I was with my uncle, for some time I began to think about leaving that country to go to some other part of the world. I did not care where I shall go to. I thought to myself that if I should get away, and go to some other country, probably I may find some comfort, more than to live there without mother and father. I thought it will be better for me to go than to stay. About his time there was a ship come from New-York—Captain Brintnall, master. As soon as it got in to the harbor, in the very place where I lived, I thought of no more but to take the best chance I had, and if the captain have no objection, to take me as one of his own servants, and to obey his word. As soon as the ship anchored I went on board. The captain soon inquired whose boy I was. Yet I know not what he says to me, for I could not speak the English language. But there was a young man who could speak English, and he told the captain that I was the minister's nephew—(the minister of that place.) The captain wished me to stay on board the ship that night, and the next day go home. This very much satisfied me, and I consented to stay. At evening, the captain invited me to eat supper with him. And there sat another boy with us who was to be my fellow-traveler, by name Thomas Hopoo—Thomas, a name given him by the supercargo of the ship. After supper the captain made some inquiry to see if we were willing to come to America; and soon I made a motion with my head that I was willing to go. This man was very agreeable, and his kindness much delighted my heart, as if I was his own son, and he was my own father. Thus I still continue thankful for his kindness toward me.

"The next morning the captain wished me to go on shore and see my uncle whether he was willing to let me go with him or not. I then got into a canoe and went on shore and found my uncle. He was at home. He asked me where was I been through all that night before. I told him that I was on board the ship, and staid there all the night. And I told him what my object was, and all what the captain invite me to. As soon as my uncle heard that I was going to leave him, he shut me up in a room, for he was not willing to let me go. While I was in the room, my old grandmother coming in asked me what was my notion of leaving him, and go with people whom I know not. I told her it is better for me to go than to stay there. She said if I should leave them I shall not see them anymore. I told her that I shall come back in a few months, if I live. Her eyes were filled with tears. She said that I was very foolish boy. This was all she said, and she went out from the room. As soon as she went out, I looked around, expecting to find a hole that I might escape out of the house. And as soon as I saw a little hole in the side of the house, I got through it and went on board the ship. When my uncle heard that I was on board the ship, he got into his canoe and came board the ship inquiring after me. No sooner had he made some inquiry but I was there discovered by one of our countrymen who had the care of the ship, and was brought forth, and come to my uncle's house. He would not let me go unless I pay him a hog for his god: (for I was taken under his care to be made for a minister.)"

Here there is an interruption in the history, and it does not appear whether the exacted price was paid or not for his discharge and permission to come to America. Permission, however, was soon obtained.

"My uncle," he says, "would not delay me no longer, and I took my leave of them and bid them farewell. My parting with them was disagreeable to them and to me, but I was willing to leave all my relations, friends, and acquaintance; expected to see them no more in this world. We set out on our journey towards the Seal-Islands, on the N.W. part of America. On these islands the captain left about twenty or thirty men for sealing-business on his way to Hawaii. We found them safe. Among these men I found a very desirable young man, by name Russel Hubbard, a son of Gen. Hubbard, of New-Haven. This

Mr. Hubbard was a member of Yale College. He was a friend of Christ. Christ as with him when I saw him, but I knew it not. 'Happy is the man that put his trust in God!' Mr. Hubbard was very kind to me on our passage, and taught me the letters in English spelling-book."

How remarkable that he should have fallen immediately into the hands of one who sought his improvement, and felt concerned for his spiritual welfare.

"We continued on these islands during six months, then took our course towards Hawaii. Two of my countrymen were with me in the ship. One of them concluded to stay at Hawaii, and the other to proceed on the voyage. The ship delayed no longer than a few days, and we set out for China on our course to America. On our way toward China, my poor friend Thomas fell overboard. He was so careless, not knowing what he was about, he went outside of the ship and drew salt-water to wash plates with (for he was a cabin's boy.) When the ship rolled he got into the water. The captain calls all hands upon the deck and ordered to have all the sails pull down in order to let about. While we were working upon our sails, my friend Thomas was out of sight. While he was in the water he pulls all off his clothes in order to be lighter. We turned out ship and went back after him. We found him almost dead. He was in the water two and a half hours. O how glad was I then to see him—for I thought he was already gone.

"We took our direct course from hence as it was before. Soon we landed at an island belonging to that part of China, and in the evening after the sundown we anchored. On the next morning we fired one of our cannon for a pilot. When we had fired once or twice, there was another ship of war belonging to the British, which stood about four or five miles apart from us. As soon as they heard our cannon they sent of their brigs. We were then taken by it for a while. They took our captain and he went on board the ship of war. He was there for a number of days. After this the Englishmen agreed to let us go. We therefore leave that place, called Mocow (Macao) and direct our course to the city of Canton. We were there until we sold out all our seal-skins and loaded our ship with other sort of goods, such as tea, cinnamon, nankeens, and silk. At the end of six months we steered a direct course to America.

"At the Cape of Good Hope, or before it, our sailors on board the ship began to terrify us. They said that there was a man named

Neptune who lived in that place, and his abiding-place was in the sea. In the evening the sailors begun the act. One of them took an old great coat and put on him, and with a speaking-trumpet in his hand, and his head was covered with a sheep-skin; and he went forward of the ship and making a great noise. About this time friend Thomas and myself were on the quarter-deck, hearing some of them telling about Neptune's coming with an iron canoe and iron paddle. Friend Thomas questioned whether the iron canoe will not sink down in the water. 'No,' said some of them, 'he will make it light, for he is a god.' While we were talking, the first we heard the sound of trumpet as follows:

" 'Ship hail! From whence came you?'

" 'The captain immediately giving an answer in this manner: 'From Canton.'

" 'Have you got my boys,' said the old Neptune.

" 'Yes,' answered the captain.

" 'How many boys have you?' added the old Neptune.

" 'Two,' said the captain, (that is myself and friend Thomas.)

"As soon as we both heard the captain says 'two,' we both scared almost to death, and wished that we were at home. The old Neptune wished to see us, but we dare not come near at it. He continued calling us to come to him, or else he would take both of us to be as his servants. We therefore went up immediately and shook our hands with him in friendly manner. I thought that he was quiet an old age, by seeing his long beards and his head covered with gray hairs; for his head was covered with a sheep-skin. After our conversation with him he wished for drink. So that I went and filled two pails full of salt-water, (as the sailors had told us,) and I set them before him. Then he took his speaking-trumpet and put it in my mouth for tunnel, in order to make me drink that salt-water which I brought. But while he stoops down to reach the pail of water, I took hold of the speaking-trumpet and hold it on one side of my cheek, so that I may not drink a drop of salt-water: did not anybody knew it, for it was dark. Bur friend Thomas he was so full of scare, he took down the whole pail of salt-water. On the next morning he was taken sick, and puked from the morning until the evening.

"About this time our provision was almost out. We had no bread, meat and water, save only one biscuit a day, and one pint of water only when the cook put in our tea. We were looking out for a vessel for a long time. Within a few days we come close to a schooner going to the West Indies, sailed from Boston. We fired at her in order to stop her.

She did so. We got from them as much provision as we wished, and this lasted till we arrived at New-York."

CHAPTER II

RESIDENCE AT NEW-HAVEN
AND TORRINGFORD

"WE LANDED at New-York," continues Obookiah's narrative, "in the year 1809; remained there a few weeks, and after the captain sold out all the goods that are in the ship, we then parted with all our sailors—every one to go to their own home. But friend Thomas and myself continued with the captain. One evening two gentlemen called on board the ship to see us. After our conversation was made with them, they wished us to go with them into a play-house, to show the curiosity. We then went with them into the play-house and saw a great number of people, as I ever saw before. We staid during the fore part of the evening, then went on board the ship. The next morning the same two gentlemen called again and invited us to come to their house that fore-noon. So that we both went. I thought while in the house of these two gentlemen how strange to see females eat with men."

It is well for the young to understand that in the Sandwich Isles, as in all heathen countries, females were degraded, and made the servants and drudges of men. The Gospel raises them from this servitude and makes them their equals and companions.

"Within a few days we left our ship and went home with Captain Brintnall to New-Haven, the place where he lived. There I lived with him for some time. In this place I become acquainted with many students belonging to the college. By these pious students I was told more about God than what I had heard before; but I was so ignorant that I could not see into it whether it was so. Many times I wish to hear more about God, but find nobody to interpret it to me. I attended many meetings on the Sabbath, but find difficulty to understand the minister. I could understand or speak but very little of the English language.

Friend Thomas went to school to one of the students in the college before I thought of going to school. I heard that a ship was ready to sail from New-York within a few days for Hawaii. The captain was willing that I might take leave of this country and go home, if I wish.

But this was disagreeable to my mind. I wished to continue in this country a little longer. I staid another week—saw Mr. E.W. Dwight, who first taught me to read and write. The first time I saw him, he inquired whether I was one who come over with Thomas, (for Thomas was known among many scholars in college.) I told him I was one who come over with Thomas. He then asked me if I wished to learn to read and write, I told him that I was.

He wished me to come to his room that night and begin to learn. So that I went in the evening and began to read in the spelling-book. Mr. Dwight wished me to come to his room at any time when it is agreeable to the captain with whom I then lived. I went home that night, and the next morning I mentioned all this matter to the captain. He was pleased, and he wished me to go to school to Dwight. Thus I continued in school with him for several months."

When Obookiah was first discovered at New-Haven, his appearance was unpromising. He was clothed in a rough sailor's suit, was of a clumsy form, and his countenance dull and heavy. His friend has almost determined to pass him by, as one whom it would be in vain to notice and attempt to instruct. But when the question was put to him, "Do you wish to learn?" his countenance began to brighten. And when the proposal was made that he should come the next day to the college for that purpose, he seized it with great eagerness.

It was not long after he began to study, and had obtained some further knowledge of the English language, that he gave evidence that the dullness, which was thought to be indicated by his countenance, formed no part of his character. It soon appeared that his eyes were open to every thing that was passing around him, and that he had an unusual degree of discernment with regard to persons and things of every description that came within his notice. The first exhibition that was made of this trait in his character, and indeed the first decisive evidence he furnished that his mind was less inactive than had been supposed, was in the following incident:

When he began to read in words of one or two syllables in the spelling-book, there were certain sounds which he found it very difficult to articulate. This was true especially of syllables that contained the letter *R*—a letter which occasioned him more trouble than all others. In pronouncing it, he uniformly gave it the sound of *L*. At every different reading an attempt was made to correct the pronunciation. The language generally used on such occasions was,

"*Try*, Obookiah, it is *very easy*." This was often repeated. But it was soon perceived that whenever these words were used they excited a smile. And as his patience began to be tried by many unsuccessful attempts, and the words to be used more in earnest, he was observed to turn away his face for the purpose of concealment, and seemed much diverted. As he was unable to express his thoughts except by acts, no explanation was made or demanded. The reason was scarcely perceived, but as attempts to correct the error were at last successful, the circumstance was soon forgotten.

A short time after this, long enough for Obookiah to have made some improvement in speaking the English, his instructor was spending an evening pleasantly with him, in making inquiries concerning some of the habits and practices of his own country. Among other things, he mentioned the manner in which his countrymen *drank from a spring*, when out upon their hunting excursions. The cup which they used was their hands. It was made by clasping them together, and so adjusting the thumbs, and bending the hands, as to form a vessel which would contain a considerable quantity. Of this he gave an example; and after preparing his hands, was able, from the pliableness of his arms, to raise them entirely to his mouth, without turning them at all from their horizontal position. The experiment was attempted by his instructor, but he found that before his hands were raised half the distance to his mouth, they were so much inverted that their contents would have been principally lost. He repeated the trial until he began to be discouraged; when Obookiah, who had been much amused with his efforts, with a very expressive countenance said to him, *"Try, Mr. Dwight, it is very easy."* The former mystery was now unraveled, and an important lesson taught as to the ease or difficulty with which things are done by us that are or are not natural to us, or to which we have or have not, from early life, been accustomed.

About this time it was discovered that Obookiah noticed with uncommon acuteness and interest every singularity in the speech and manners of those around him; and in the midst of his own awkwardness, to the surprise of all, he suddenly began to show himself dexterous as a mimic. He one day placed himself upon the floor, drew up his sleeves half way to the elbow, walked across the room with a peculiar air; and said, *"Who dis?"* The person intended was instantly known by all that were present. He then put himself in a different position, changed his gait, and said again, *"Well, who dis?"* This imitation also was so accurate, of another of the members of college, that no one doubted as to the original. The extent of his own awkwardness at this time may be learned from the effect that an exhibition of it produced upon himself. After he had completed his own efforts at mimicry, his friend said to him, "Well, Obookiah, should you like to know how you walk?" He seemed much pleased, and the imitation was attempted. He was greatly diverted, though almost incredulous, and said with earnestness—several times repeating the question—*"Me walk so?"*

After being assured that it was a reality, he burst into a roar of laughter and fell upon the floor, where he indulged his mirth until his strength was exhausted.

The same trait of character was discoverable in the manner in which he was affected with respect to the idols of the heathen, upon the first instruction given him concerning the true God. He was at once very sensibly impressed with the *ludicrous* nature of idol worship. Smiling at its absurdity, he said "Hawaii gods! They *wood, burn*. Me go home, put'em in a fire, burn'em up. They no *see*, no *hear*, no *any thing*—then added, *"We make them—Our God,* (looking up,) *he make us."*

The history proceeds: "Now I wished no more to live with captain any longer, but rather wished to live some where else, where I could have an opportunity to learn to write and read. I went to my friend Mr. Dwight who was to be my best and kind friend; I made known to him all my desire. I told him that I wished to live where I could have an opportunity to get in some school, and work a part of the time. He then wished me to live with President Dwight. This satisfied me; I went with him to Dr. Dwight's house. I lived with this pious and good family for some time, and went to school to the same man as before. While I lived with these good people I have more time to attend to my book than I ever did before. Here was the first time I meet with praying family morning and evening. It was difficult for me to understand what was said in prayer, but I doubt not this good people were praying for me while I was with them—seeing that I was ignorant of God and of my Savior. I heard of God as often as I lived with this family, and I believed but little. Whilst I lived at Dr. Dwight's, I went up to my school-room one evening and saw Mr. Samuel J. Mills, a son of Rev. Samuel J. Mills, of Torringford, sitting with Mr. Dwight my instructor. Mr. Dwight wished me to make acquaintance with Mr. Mills. So did I—and shook hands with him. Mr. Mills continued in New-

Haven for several months. During this time he wished me to go home with him; he says he has a good father, mother, brother and sister. This requesting was very pleasing to me, so that I consented. I then left New-Haven and went home with Mr. Mills. I lived with this family in the year 1810. These people were the most judicious and kindest people. I was treated by them in the most affectionate manner—(yet not knowing who brought me there, for I was very ignorant of Him who gave me so many good friends in this country.) It seemed to me as my own home. It was. And I have made my home there frequently. I could say much of them, but what more can I do but to remember their kindness toward me? While I was with them I continued my study in spelling, reading, and writing to M. Jeremiah Mills, a brother of Mr. Mills whom I was acquainted with at the first. Here I learned some sort of farming business: cutting wood, pulling flax, mowing, &c.—only to look at the other and learn from them."

As Obookiah was to obtain, in part, his support at Mr. Mills' by his labor, he was immediately set about most kinds of business that pertain to a farm. And though this was a new employment to him, he was found to excel in every thing to which he turned his hand. One glance at others for an example was all the instruction that he required before he was ready to undertake, and to perform skillfully, every kind of labor.

The following extract of a letter from the Rev. Mr. Mills sufficiently illustrates this part of his character.

"There was something unusual in regard to Obookiah. His attention to what passed before him, and his talent at imitation, were singular. He had never mown a clip until he came to live with me. My son furnished him with a scythe. He stood and looked on to see the use he made of it, and at once followed, to the surprise of those who saw him. A number of hands also engaged in reaping. We furnished him with a sickle. He stood and looked, and followed on. It was afterwards observed by a person who was in the field, that there were not two reapers there who excelled him.

"In these respects and others he was truly a remarkable youth."

While Obookiah remained in the family of Mr. Mills "every possible attention was paid to the improvement of his mind, and his progress was such as to convince those who instructed him that their labor was not in vain. He soon acquired knowledge of the spelling-book, and in a few months was able to read in the Testament. By this time he had also made considerable proficiency in writing. It was observed that he learned to talk English just as fast as he learned to read it. When he became able to communicate his ideas in a broken manner, he would express a very tender concern for his countrymen."

Henry now made his first essay at letter-writing. His first letter was written to his friend Thomas at New-Haven, and the second to his former instructor. The last has been preserved, and for reasons that will be obvious, is here inserted. The following is an exact copy:

"Torringford, March 2, 1810.

"Mr. E.D.—Sir

"I here now—this place, Torringford—I glad see you very much. I laugh Tom Hoboo—he says—"Obooki write me that? Me no write." I want you tell Tom, Mr. S. Mills say if we be good boys we shall have friends. One morning you know I come into your room in college, and you tell me—*read—you say, what c.a.p. spell? then I say c.a.p. pig.* I spell four syllables now, and I say what is the chief end of man. I like you much. I like your brother and your friend Mr. Dean. I wear this great-coat you gave me to meeting every Sunday. I wish you would write me a letter and tell me what Tom do.

"This from

"HENRY OBOOKI."

"Mrs. Mills, the wife of the Rev. Mr. Mills." Continues Obookiah, "was a very amiable woman and I was treated by her as her own child. She used me kindly and learned me to say Catechism.

"Many ministers called on the Rev. Mr. Mills, and I was known by a great number of ministers. But on account of my ignorance of God, I do not wish to hear them when they talk to me. I would not wish to be in the room where they were; neither did I wish to come near a minister, for the reason that he should talk to me about God, whom I hated to hear. I was told by them about heaven and hell, but I did not pay any attention to what they say; for I thought that I was just as happy as the other people, as those who do know about God much more than I do. But this thought, as I see it now, was the most great and dangerous mistake."

Here let us not fail to notice, as illustrating divine truth, the natural aversion of the human heart to God. Notwithstanding the amiable character of this youth, and his eagerness to receive instruction on every other subject, he was unwilling to be talked to about God, whom he hated to hear. Let others see themselves as in a glass, and seek that happy change which Obookiah early sought and found.

CHAPTER III

RESIDENCE AT ANDOVER
AND VICINITY

"AT THE CLOSE of the year 1810," he says, I left Torringford and went to Andover. I continued there for some time. Here my wicked heart began to see a little about the divine things; but the more I see to it, the more it appear to be *impenetrability*. I took much satisfaction in conversing with many students in the institution. I spent a little time with some of them and in going to one room and to another to recite to them, for I was taken under their care. Whenever I got a lesson I had a right to go to any room in college to recite. While I was there, for a long time, my friend Mr. Mills was there; one of my kindest friends that I had, who took me away from his father's house. This young Mr. Mills was studying divinity at the college when I was instructed by the students."

It was at this time, and with the friend who has been mentioned, that Obookiah made his first attempt to pray in the presence of another. His friend, having knelt down and prayed, turning to him before they rose, said, "You may pray." When he expressed himself substantially in the following terms.

"Great and eternal God—make heaven—make earth—make every thing—have mercy on me—make me understand the Bible—make me good—great God have mercy on Thomas—make him good—make Thomas and me go back to Hawaii—tell folks in Hawaii no more pray to stone god—make some good man go with me to Hawaii, tell folks in Hawaii about heaven—about hell—God make all people good every where—great God have mercy on college—make all good—make Mr. Samuel good—have mercy on Mr. Samuel's father, mother, sister, brother. 'Our Father which art in heaven; Hallowed be thy name. Thy kingdom come. Thy will be done in earth, as it *is* in heaven. Give us this day our daily bread. And forgive us our debts as we forgive our debtors. And lead us not into temptation; but deliver us from evil. For thine is the kingdom, and the power, and the glory, for ever. Amen.' "

"My friend Mr. Mills now thought it would be well for me to leave Andover and go to some school where I may improve my time much more than I could there. He said if I should go he would try to find some good people who would be willing to support me. This was a most kind offer, which I cannot feel any more than to be thankful for all this kindness to me. Mr. Mills now sent me to Bradford Academy; and there I continued for some time at school. The people where I boarded at the house of Deacon Hasseltine, (the family of Mrs. Judson, Missionary to Burmah,) were a most pious family. But while I was here in the school my serious feelings, which I had before, I lost all; and become very ignorant of religion by being among some *unserious* company, talking many foolish subjects. I thought now I shall never have any more such feelings as I had before—I thought that I must always be miserable here and hereafter. I become prayerless and thoughtless—no hope for mercy—never attempted to be alone as I had done before. I sit and walked about all day—took no opportunity to be at the throne of grace, but rather to be stupid—from the morning until evening never thought of Him who kept me alive, neither when I lay down upon my bed, not when I rose up. I was in this situation for a long time while I was at school. At the close of the school I went back to Andover. Mr. Mills was not there. It was vacation, I staid until he returned. When he returned he inquired how I have been, and how I was pleased with the school. I answered, well. But I did not let him know what was my situation, and what trouble I had met with while I was there, but kept all these things in my own mind.

"In the spring season of the year 1811, I hired myself out for a month or two, on account of my health, with Mr. F. who lived about five miles from the college. Mr. F. one day sent me into the woods not far from the house to work. I took an axe and went and worked there till towards noon. But here O, I come to myself again! many thoughts come into my mind that I was in a dangerous situation. I thought if I should then die I must certainly be cast off for ever. While I was working it appeared as it was a voice saying 'Cut it down, why cumbereth it the ground.' I worked no longer—but dropped my axe, and walked a few steps from the place (for the people in the house would soon send a lad after me, for it was noon.) I fell upon my knees and looked up to the Almighty Jehovah for help. I was not but an undone and hell-deserving sinner. I felt that it would be just that God should cast me off whithersoever he would—that he should do with my poor soul as it seemed to him fit. I spent some time here until I heard a boy calling for me—and I went. The people in the house asked of my sadness—to which I give but little answer. In the night my sleep was taken away from me. I kept awake almost the whole night. Many of my feelings and thoughts in past time came into remembrance—and how I treated the mercy of God while I was at Bradford Academy. The next morning I rose up before the rest, and went to a place where I was alone by myself. Here I went both morning, night, and noon. At this place I find some comfort. And when I go there I enjoy myself better all the day.

"At the end of two months I returned to Andover. Many times Mr. Mills asked me about my feelings, and I was neither willing to answer much, nor could I on account of my unfaithfulness and wickedness.

"I continued here a few days and then hired myself out again, and went to labor for Mr. A. a farmer, in haying time. Mr. A. was a good man, and it was a religious family. I had here the same seriousness in my mind as before, but never did meet with real change of heart yet."

During Obookiah's residence at Andover he lived two years in the family of Mr. Abbot, the steward of the Theological Institution. This family bears very favorable testimony to the excellence of his character. They speak of him with tears. Said Mrs. Abbot to a friend, "He was always pleasant. I never saw him angry. He used to come into my chamber and kneel down by me and pray. Mr. Mills did not think he was a Christian at that time, but he appeared to be thinking of nothing else but religion. He afterwards told me that there was a time when he wanted *to get religion into his head more than into his heart."*

In an absence of a month of two from the family, he wrote a letter to Mrs. Abbot, from which the following is an extract.

"I sometimes think about my poor soul, and that which God hath done. I will cry unto God—'What shall I do to be saved?' I know that God is able to take away blind eyes and wicked heart, we must be born again and have a new spirit before we die. As soon as we shall be dead, all we must stand before the judgment-seat of Christ. Friend, perhaps you have not done any thing wicked, so that God can punish you. I hope you have not. But if we are not his friends and followers he will cast us into hell, and we shall be there for ever and ever. I hope you will think upon all these things. Friend to you,

HENRY OBOOKIAH."

Whilst at Andover Obookiah heard that one of his countrymen resided in the vicinity. He hastened to him and spent a part of the day with him, and a night, in which they did not sleep. When he returned, a friend said to him, "Well, Henry, what news from Hawaii? He replied, *"I did not think of Hawaii, I had so much to say about Jesus Christ."*

Henry had now become diligent in studying the Scriptures, and made rapid progress in religious knowledge. The following fact is a specimen of what he had attained.

He was asked, "How many miracles are recorded of our Savior?" He began with the first, that of making water wine, and mentioned them all. Can others of his age do this, who have had opportunity to know the Savior's history much longer, and been better able to read it?

In a letter from Andover communicating the preceding facts, it is observed, Mr. Abbot, the steward, says, "Henry was very inquisitive, and could never be satisfied until he saw the whole of a subject. It was peculiarly observable during an eclipse of the sun, concerning which he asked many troublesome questions; and also with regard to many kinds of public business; particularly the mode of levying, collecting and appropriating taxes."

"He was seen one morning very early with a rule measuring the college buildings and fences. He was asked why he did it. He smiled and said, 'So that I shall know how to build when I go back to Hawaii.' "When he heard a word," said Mr. Abbot, "which he did not understand or could not speak, it was his constant habit to ask me, 'How you *spell?* how you spell?' When I told him he never forgot."

The same letter observes, "Henry's *playfulness and ingenuity* have ever been to me a most interesting trait in his character. He went into the steward's kitchen one evening and tied, secretly, a thread to one of the posts of a chair in which a person sat, and then seated himself in a back part of the room. He said to the family sitting about the fire, "Look, look." In the middle of floor were seen two little gentlemen dancing— shaking their feet and fists and at last fighting. In the contest one fell, then the other. At last they got up in very good nature and jumped into Henry's pocket.

"He had seen such an exhibition at some stopping-place on his voyage to America."

Henry now began to maintain a correspondence with his absent friends:—a practice in which he seemed to take unusual pleasure through the whole of his future life.

The two following letters, written at Andover, were exactly copied from the original, with a few corrections in the punctuation.

Andover, Dec. 15, 1812.
"Dear Christian Friend,

"I improve this opportunity to write to you. And I saw your beloved book which you sent by Mr. G. and that I very much thank you for it. I am great joy to God to give me such a good friend in this land where we hear the words of God—God is kind to us and to the other—that is to every body else God will carry through his work for us.

"I do not know what will God do with my poor soul. I shall go before God and also both Christ.

"We must all try to get forward where God wish us to do. God is able to save sinners if we have some feeling in him. Is very great thing to have hope in him, and do all the christian graces. I hope the Lord will send the Gospel to the Heathen land where the words of the Savior never yet had been. Poor people worship the wood, and stone, and shark, and almost every thin their gods; the Bible is not there, and heaven and hell they do not know about it. I yet in this country and no father and no mother. But God is friend if I will do his will, and not my own will."

The following letter was written to the Rev. Mr. Mills, of Torringford.

"Andover, Jan. 27, 1813.

"Very dear Christian Friend,

"I improve this opportunity to write to you a letter. I received your two letters, and I had broken the seals of both of them, and I have read those sweet words that make my poor and wicked heart feel cold, as like cold water. O Lord, how long shall I continue in my own sins? Lord, wilt thou hear my secret prayer?

"Dear sir, I hope your prayer for the poor and blind immortal souls will be heard. I thank you to pray for me beside my own prayer. Pray to God that he might pour down his Holy Spirit upon all our souls. I do not know what will become of my poor soul when my time is full come hereafter. But in my own feeling I wish his will, and I am willing that God do what he please for my poor soul. What are sweet things in this world, sinners like better than their own souls which are going down to the bottomless pit. O how wicked and sinful are we. How shall we go the path of life and of his truth, and to be with him in heaven? No way at all; only we must give away ourselves to him and leave all our sins behind. Some think they know not how to pray; but they ought to know, for Christ hath taught us, I went to Tyngsbury last week to see a boy who came from Hawaii. He arrived last June—(this is not Thomas that came with me.) As the distance from this place was small, I went to visit him. I hope the Lord will have mercy upon his poor soul. He knew nothing of the Savior before I told him. I first mentioned to him Genesis I. &c. telling him that God made the world by his own power; then he said, 'O how foolish we are to worship wood and stone gods; we give them hogs, and cocoa nuts, and banana, but they cannot eat.' Yes, said I, it is foolish. Then he asked me where that man was that made every thing. I told him he was every where with us. Does he hear when you and I talk? says he. I told him yes, and you must believe in him if you would be his friend. He said he did believe what I told him. He has not learned to understand English, but I spoke in Hawaii. I took him with me to the minister's house on Sabbath evening, so I told him in Hawaii what Mr. Allen the minister said, He had been before, but could not understand what was said. I told him what God did for him in keeping him alive, and bringing him t this country. He said he liked that man very much, (meaning God.) He asked me many questions again and again about God, which I answered. After we went to bed he said he never would forget what I had told him. He said when he eat he would remember who gave him food. The people where he lived said he might stay there as he would; and when he had learned English a little, he might go to school. He did cry when I left him."

In the spring of the year 1812, Mr. Mills, the particular patron of Obookiah at this period, was appointed by the American Board of Commissioners for Foreign Missions, to take a missionary tour through the Western and Southern States. Soon after his departure Obookiah went to spend several months at Hollis, in New-Hampshire. "Here," he says, "I lived with two good men, Dea. E. and Dea. B. and with the Rev. Mr. S. While I was in this place I became more thoughtful about myself. I attended many of the young people's meetings, and I was quite happy. But I was now taken sick of a fever at the house of Dea. B. I was very weak, and was not able to answer to the questions of those who come to visit me. Then I thought I, where shall I go for a physician, but unto thee! Death had but a little fear. I continued sick for five weeks. The whole family of Dea. B. were very kind. I was treated with the most affectionate care during the whole of my sickness. Doctor C. was a very kind and friendly man. He was a pious and good Christian. Many times he prayed with me while I was upon my sick bed.

"One day Mrs. B. asked me whether I was willing to die and leave this world of sin and go to the better. To which I replied that I should have no objection if God should do with me as it seemed to him fit. She added, 'Do you remember the goodness and the kindness of God towards you?' I answered yes—for I have neither a father nor a mother, nor a brother nor a sister in this strange country but he. But O! am I fit to call him my Father? 'Whosoever doeth his will, the same is a child of God.' No longer after my complaint was over I began to experience hope in religion. I thought often concerning the happiness of another world and eternal realities. But my mind and my heart of wickedness would often turn back to this world, (if I do not think about the serious things.) Many times I meet with dark hour. But the greatest part of the time I took much comfort and happiness, both in my secret prayer and in serious conversation with others. I thought now with myself had I have met with a change of heart. It was so, if I mistake not. *For the Lord Jesus did appear as chiefest among ten thousand and altogether lovely; and his mercy appeared to be welcome to a sinner as I.*"

It was during this residence at Hollis, in all probability, and perhaps in this season of sickness, that Henry's heart was renewed by the Holy Spirit. He had not in his own view obtained mercy previously to this; but now he began "to experience hope in religion," and to give evidence of a spiritual and heavenly mind.

Now the decisive proof of true conversion began to appear:—*a supreme regard for the Savior—an apprehension of is infinite excellence and loveliness, and of his perfect and wonderful adaptedness to the wants of "a poor sinner."*

If the young convert would think less of himself and far more of Christ, and dwell upon his loveliness, glory and sufficiency, and consecrate the *whole* soul immediately to him forever, serving no cherished sins, there would be few "fears and doubts;" and if this were made the test of true conversion as it should be, there would be little danger of false and delusive hopes of heaven.

In the fall, Henry left Hollis and returned to Andover, where he remained until the succeeding spring; when he took his final leave of the place and went "home" to the house of the Rev. Mr. Mills, in Torringford.

CHAPTER IV

PUBLIC PROFESSION OF CHRIST— DEVOTION TO THE MISSIONARY WORK

DURING THIS residence at Mr. Mills' he occasionally visited Litchfield, to see the person who had been his early friend at New-Haven. As this was but a short period after his hopeful conversion, his friend was anxious to ascertain what knowledge he possessed of experimental religion. To the questions that were asked him, he gave answers which clearly evinced that on this subject he had thought and felt for himself; and furnished as much reason to hope that the had been savingly instructed by the Holy Spirit. "How does your own heart appear to you?" was a question put to him. To which he replied, *"O black, very black."* But you hope you have a new heart, how did it appear to you before it was changed?" *"Mud,"* he said, *"all mud."*

His conversation was at this time much upon the subject of religion, and he seemed, for so young a Christian, to be in an uncommon degree heavenly minded. He said, "When I at home—Torringford out in the field, I can't help think about heaven. I go in a meadow—work at the hay—my hands—but my thought—no there. *In heaven—all the time—* then I very happy."

He had already acquired a very considerable knowledge of the Scriptures. He quoted passages appropriate to almost every subject of conversation. It was evident that his mind dwelt upon the truths of the Bible, and that he found much of his habitual pleasure in searching out the less obvious treasures which it contained. He manifested great inquisitiveness with regard to passages of Scripture, the meaning of which he did not entirely comprehend. Many passages were the subject of inquiry. "What our Saviour mean," said he, "when he say, 'In my Father's house are many mansion—I go prepare a place for you.' 'What he mean, *'I go prepare a place?"*

The readiness and propriety with which he quoted passages of Scripture on every occasion were particularly noticed by all who conversed with him. In one of his visits he asked his friend, who was now in the study of divinity, to go aside with him, as if he had something of importance which he wished to reveal. But it appeared that it was his object to converse with him upon the subject of accompanying him to the Sandwich Islands. He plead with great earnestness that he would go and preach the gospel to his poor countrymen. Not receiving so much encouragement as he desired, he suspected that his friend might be influenced by the fear of the consequences of attempting to introduce a new religion amongst the heathen. Upon which, though he had now just begun to lisp the language of the Scriptures, he said, *"You fraid?* You know our Savior say, *'He that will save his life shall lose it; and he that will lose his life for my sake, same shall save it.'* "

His own fearlessness and zeal on this subject he exhibited about the same time to an aged minister, who asked him why he wished to return. He replied—"To preach the Gospel to my countrymen." He was asked what he would say to them about their wooden god. He answered, "Nothing." "But," said the clergyman, "suppose your countrymen should tell you that preaching Jesus Christ was blaspheming their gods, and should put you to death?" To this he replied with great emphasis, "If that be the will of God, *I am ready, I am ready.*"

In the fall of 1813 Henry was invited by James Morris, Esq. of Litchfield, to spend the winter in his family and attend the public grammar school, of which for many years he had been preceptor. Here Henry commenced the study of English grammar, geography and arithmetic, in which he made during the winter very considerable progress. In the spring of 1814 he returned to Mr. Mills' and spent the summer principally in laboring on the farm. At the annual meeting of the North Consociation of Litchfield County, in the fall of 1814, Henry, by the advice of his friends, applied to that body to take him under their care, and give him counsel and direction as to his studies and other concerns. The Consociation voted to comply with his request, and appointed a board, consisting of three persons, to superintend his education, and report to the Consociation annually.

After Obookiah was taken under the care of the Consociation he pursued his studies under the direction of their committee, so far as the charity of his Christian friends furnished him with the means. He was obliged to labor a part of the time for his own support, and to change from time to time his place of residence. The evidences of his Christian character, in the view of those who had most opportunity to serve him, were continually brightening. He discovered a strong relish for the

Bible, was constant in reading it, and seldom would any object or circumstances prevent his reading daily some portion of the Scriptures. Occasionally, when requested, he has prayed and spoken in social religious meetings; and always performed those services to the acceptance, and, it is believed, to the edification of those present.

The summer of 1814 Henry spent at Torringford. "In the beginning of summer," he says, "my friend Mr. Mills, whom I loved, returned from his Missionary tour. I received him with joyful salutation. Several times he asked me how my wicked heart get along while I was hoeing corn. But I was still fearful to tell whether my heart was changed or not.

"At this time Mr. Mills wished me to go and live with the Rev. Mr. Harvey, of Goshen. This was pleasing to me, and I went to live with him and studied geography and mathematics; and a part of the time was trying to translate a few verses of the Scriptures into my own language, and in making a kind of spelling-book, taking the English alphabet and giving different names and different sounds—(for this language was not written language.) I spent some time in making a kind of spelling-book, dictionary, grammar.

"While I was in this place with Rev. Mr. Harvey I took more happiness upon my knees than I ever did before, having a good room to study and being alone the greatest part of the time. Many happy and serious thoughts were coming into my mind while I was upon my bed in the night. Every thing appeared to be very clear to my own view. Many times the Lord Jesus appeared in my mind to be the most great and glorious. O what happy hours that I had in the night season! I thought sometimes before, that religion was a hard thing to get it— making many excuses for *pray hour,* and kept putting off from time to time, and thought that it would become easier some time at hand. But this kind of feeling led me far beyond all happiness. Many times I lived as a man that travels up to a hill and then down. But it was nothing that hindered me but my own wicked heart, and because I did not repent for my sin.

"I seeked for the Lord Jesus for a long time, but found him not. It was because I did not seek him in a right manner. But still I do think that I have found him upon my knees. *The Lord was not in the wind, neither in the earthquake, nor in the fire, but in still small voice.*

"About this time I thought with myself to join with some church. I wished to give every thing up for the glory of God, to give up my whole soul to him, to do with me as he pleaseth. I made known these things to the Rev. Mr. Harvey, and he thought it would be better for me to make a profession of the religion. He wished me to go and see the Rev. Mr. Mills and the people whom I have been acquainted with and talk the matter over with them; for I longed to be. I therefore went and conversed with my good friend and father Mills concerning my case. All the matter seemed to him well. He wished me to come over on the next Sabbath and attend my examination. I staid at Goshen until the approaching of the Sabbath which was appointed, and then went over to Torringford. I thought while I was travelling, that I was going home to New Jerusalem—to the welcome gate. As I walked along I repeated these words, 'Whom have I in heaven but thee? and there is none upon the earth that I desire besides thee.' I was received into the church of Christ in Torringford, on the ninth day of April in the year 1815. The following is the text which the Rev Mr. Mills preached from: 'I will bring the blind by a way that they know not; I will lead them in paths that they have not known.' "

Previously to the time appointed for the admission of Obookiah into the church, he requested Mr. Mills to give him an opportunity, if he thought it proper, at the time of his admission, "to speak a few word to the people." Mr. Mills readily consented—but from some particular circumstances, he did not recollect, at the proper time, Henry's request, and it was neglected. After the public services were closed and Mr. Mills had retired to his study, Henry went to him with a broken heart, and said, "You no let me speak, sir—I sorry." Mr. Mills was much affected but there was no remedy. But, said he, "What did you wish to say, Henry?" He replied, "I want to ask the people what they all waiting for?—they live in Gospel land—hear all about salvation—God ready, Christ ready—all ready—Why they don't come to follow Christ?"

Although Henry became a member of the church at Torringford, he still continued his residence with the Rev. Mr. Harvey at Goshen. "Here," he says, "I lived a little more than a year, and was treated with the most affectionate and kindest treatment. I was now taken under the care of the Board of Commissioners for Foreign Missions, with a view to my future employment to be as a Missionary to my poor countrymen—who are yet living in a region and shadow of death—without knowledge of the true God and ignorant of the future world—have no Bible to read—no Sabbath—and all these things are unknown to them. With them I feel, and expected to spend the remaining part of my days in the service of our glorious Redeemer, if the Almighty should spare my life. I often feel for them in the night season concerning the loss of their souls, and wish many times to be among them before I am fit to come to them—for I long to see them. O that the Lord would pluck them from the everlasting burning! and that the Lord may be their God, and may they be his people—and be made 'partakers of the inheritance of the saints in light.' O what a happy time I have now, while my poor friends and relations at home are perishing wit hunger, and thirsty, wanting of Divine mercy and water out of the well of salvation. May the Lord Jesus dwell in my heart and prepare me to go and spend the remaining part of my life with them. But *not my will*, O Lord, *but thy will be done.* May I live with them as a stranger and pilgrim upon the earth as long as I live; and spend and be spent in the service of the Redeemer. May the Lord teach me to live in his fear, to do his will, and to live devoted to his service."

CHAPTER V

LETTERS AND DIARY

WHILE RESIDING at Goshen, he thus wrote to a friend, April 24, 1815:

"_____, I knew not what was my business when at first time I set out from home—only a boy's notion. Because I have no father or mother, I therefore thought of it, I must go and see the world, and see what I can find. I never heard any thing about Jesus, and heaven, and hell. Well, after I heard about these things, I heard that Jesus was the Son of God, and that he has come into the world to save sinners; the evil spirit then coming into my mind, and said that there was none, neither heaven nor hell. I could not believe it. Sometimes when some good people talked with me on this subject, I was but just hate to hear it.

"I hope that you and I may meet, though at present unknown to each other, in the eternal world; where many come from the east and from the west, and from the north and from the south, and sit down together in the kingdom of Christ. But I do sometimes think often that I shall never see that holy and happy world. I am very afraid, because I was a great enemy to God, and have fought against his grace and his loving-kindness towards me.

"O! my dear friend, do not forget to pray for me before our heavenly Father when you are alone. Pray for me, and for my poor countrymen, and for others, that we may escape from the wrath to come. Those that have been faithful to the Lord Jesus Christ, the same shall be saved; and those that have done evil shall come to the resurrection of damnation.

"There is no great consequence wherever we may be called, if we only keep our hearts right before God. We are under peculiar obligation to consecrate ourselves wholly to the glory of God. But we know that our deceitful hearts are apt to run down, *even as a clock or watch is*. A good clock will keep good time by winding it up; but if we don't, it certainly will run down. For 'this people,' said our Savior, 'draweth nigh unto me with their mouth, and honoreth me with their lips, but their heart is far from me.' My wicked heart has been just as those clocks which run down very often. But I hope I love the Lord Jesus Christ. I am willing to give up every thing, both my soul and body, for time and eternity. God can do all this. 'I can do all things,' said the apostle, 'through Christ,' &c.

"My dear friend, do not forget to pray for William, pray that he may ever have joy in the holy presence of God, and may he be made a good soldier of the cross of Christ. There is reason to hope that his heart will be changed, for God will have mercy on whom he will. I wish that he could live with me, so that I could do all what I can for him. God in his holy providence has brought hi and me from the heathen land. Because of the weakness of our faith and our selfishness, the gold and silver are tempting to the soul. O! can sinners expect to walk the golden streets without a perfect heart; or how shall we live with him without being born again.

"There is no way I can see for sinners but to go to Christ. 'I am the way, the truth, and the life. No man cometh unto the Father but by me,' said the Savior. 'At that day shall ye know that I am in the Father, and ye in me, and I in you.' The Lord Jesus is all ready and waiting for sinners, and inviting them to come to him immediately without delay.

"May the Lord direct you, and make you a faithful laborer in the Lord's vineyard."

The following extracts are form a letter written to the Rev. Eleazer T. Fitch, at New-Haven, dated,

"Goshen, June 4, 1815.

"My dear Friend,

"I received your kind letter, which came into my hand this day, with great pleasure. You desire me to let you know the present state of my feelings. I have no objection, but I have not much to say on this subject. You know when I was at Andover, there I was in full concern about my soul, and knew then that I was but a dying worm of the dust, and I knew I was poor sinner. And now I hope that the Lord Jesus will be my eternal portion, and direct me evermore. I have nothing to do but to be thankful for all the privileges and blessings which I enjoy. I know that God will have mercy on whom he will—and with such promise, our souls must rest in God.

"O my dear friend, do not cease to pray for me, and for Tennooe, and for the poor ignorant people at Hawaii: and pray for the poor people in this country as well as the heathen, for their hearts are not with God, and their ears are much deafer than that of the heathen— when they hear the word of God on every Sabbath and can read the Holy Scriptures. O may the Lord bless us all with an increase of his grace. I hope you will never forget to write to me when you can, and tell me what religious experience you know I am ignorant of.

"I want to see you about Grammar: I want to get through with it. I have been translating a few chapters of the Bible in to the Hawaiian language. I found I could do it very correctly.

"I hope that the great God will be gracious to you, and make you a faithful minister of the Gospel of Jesus Christ. 'Walk by faith, and not by sight.' "

Extracts from a letter to Mr. Samuel B. Ingersoll, a member of Yale College.

"Goshen, June 9, 1815.

"My dear Friend,

"I improve this opportunity to write you a few lines. When you was up here last, you know that I was quite unwell then. On that account I could not talk much with you when you was speaking on the religious subjects.

"O my friend, what is our rule? Is not the word of God, which is contained in the Scriptures of the Old and New Testament? Certainly it is. But we arc apt to hate to put away sins, for they are sweeter than the grace of God.

"O my dear friend, let us continue in the hope of the glory of our Redeemer, with true hearts in full assurance of faith. Cease not to pray for the fatherless, as I am. O what a wonderful thing it is that the hand of the Divine Providence has brought me here from that heathenish darkness where the light of divine truth never had been. And here have I found the name of the Lord Jesus in the Holy Scriptures, and have read that his blood was shed for many; and I remember his own words which he said, 'Father, forgive them, for they know not what they do.'

"Do not forget to mention me and Tennooe before our Heavenly Father when you are alone by yourself, that we may not enter into temptation, and that our souls may have rest in God. I hope to hear from you before long. When you write to me, if agreeable to you, I wish you to give me some information of religious experience, &c. and how a Christian feels, &c. &c. I hope that the Lord will be with you;

and may your journey through this vale of tears be sweetened by the precious religion of the blessed Savior. May he who is rich in mercy, and abundant in grace and goodness, bless you with an increase of his mercy, and make you a faithful soldier of the cross of Christ."

In another letter to one of his countrymen residing at Boston, he says:

"I doubt not that you have seen some people in this country, as much as I0, 20, 30, 40, 50, and 60 years of age, still neglecting religion from year to year; and adding sin to sin as long as they live. This will not do, for God hath said, 'My Spirit shall not always strive with man.' But alas, sin is a lovely friend to a sinner. He will not get away from his sins for a thousand worlds. 'O,' sinner, *'taste and see that the Lord is good.'*

"Do write me a long letter without delay, and tell me *how God did appear to you at first,* and tell me what is your first object if you should return home, &c."

The letter which follows was written to a young gentleman in Middlebury:

"Goshen, Sept. 25, 1814.

"Dear Friend,

"It is long since I saw you when you had kept Mr. B's store at Torringford; you are by no means forgotten. I conclude that you are probably in the best place. I am contented. Undoubtedly your present situation affords the best opportunity to pursue your studies; and is hoped that you have also good religious instructions and cautions. I hope you remember that the true friend of God may have pleasure wherever they are, if they make it their chief concern to glorify, love, and please him; but those who do not, have no right to expect pleasure any where. In whatever place we are, we have much that we can and ought to do for God. Our first care should be to keep our own thoughts right. We should think much on that great and holy Being that formed us; on his holiness and abhorrence of every sin; on our constant dependence upon him; how many blessings he is conferring upon us, and how little we deserve them, and how undone and unthankful we are for them; or our deserving evil instead of good, and how abominable we are in his sight whenever we do evil. We should think often on death and our appearing before the eternal Savior in judgment. We ought not only to read the Bible often, but to pray often, that we may know of the salvation, and understand and be assisted to live according to it; and this would aid us very much in keeping our thoughts. If we exercise sufficient care over our thoughts, our outward conduct also will be good. But if we employ our minds one moment on foolish our useless things, we shall not only offend God by that, but we shall be liable to fall into outward sins, and so endanger our own souls, and encourage others in the same evil; and their wickedness will encourage others, and so on. We cannot conceive the dreadful consequences of one sin, and we are very apt to forget how prone we are to fall into sin. We are very apt likewise to satisfy ourselves with what we intend to do hereafter, and to forget our present duty. The truth is, all our time is made up of present time, and all we need to care is, that we may all the time do the best we can for our great Creator this present minute. All that we can possibly do is but a little; for all we have and all we are is God's, and we can never atone for one of all our sins, but we must trust altogether in the merits of Christ. But now, my dear friend, I hope you will strive to improve all your time well, and that God will be gracious to you, and make you faithful and useful as long as you live here in the world.

"I wish you would write to me as you can. I concluded to be here with Mr. Harvey this winter; and whenever you come this way, I should be glad to see you here. Mr. and Mrs. Harvey, they are very agreeable and kind; I was very much pleased with them. I saw your father at Torringford some time ago; he wished me to write to you when I could; I told him I would.

"One thing I must mention to you, that is, we must always continue in our prayers before our heavenly Father, that we may all become followers of those who, through faith and patience, inherit the promises. But now I must close this subject.

"Your affectionate friend,

"HENRY OBOOKIAH."

In October, *1815*, Obookiah left Goshen and went to reside in the family of the Rev. Mr. Prentice, of Canaan. At this period his history of his past life terminates. He commenced writing it soon after he removed to Canaan, at the request of his instructor, as a daily exercise. It was completed in the beginning of the succeeding year. In March, he commenced a Diary, which he continued till the close of the summer;

when he changed again his place of residence, went to South Farms, and soon afterward to Amherst, in Massachusetts. From this time his situation and the nature of his employment were such that the Diary was wither suspended, or continued only at intervals, and not preserved.

The following are extracts from the Diary.

"*March 5, 1816.* This evening I attended a conference at the House of Dea. B. It was a very solemn time. Many appeared to be very serious and attentive; though I was in fear it was not so in the heart. Rev. Mr. Prentice made some observations from these words, 'Why sit we here until we die?' By hearing these words my mind was much concerned, and I felt as though I was still in my own sin. 'What shall I do?' said I to myself. The answer was, *work faithfully with your own heart.* With these thoughts coming into my mind, I found peace and joy. O that I might understand the work of my own heart.

"6. I have just now been thinking of the prophet Elijah: how he prayed to his God when he went up to the top of the Mount Carmel, and how he put his face between his knees and prayed to the God of heaven. O, how much better it is to spend time now in such a way of praying, than to wait until the time of prayer may be over. What should hinder the heart from being busy in prayer to God secretly, while the hands are full of any business whatever?

"8. This day is very dark. My mind has been quite down by reason of my barrenness. But Christ has appeared as 'chiefest among ten thousand and altogether lovely.' In Christ have I found the light of comfort and joy. Whatever joy and comfort I received from God, my heart is bound up with thanks; but at the other time I become forgetful, as if I was carrying away by my own sin, as far as where it was not to be remembered what God had one for my soul.

"9. I have had this morning a solemn visit from two young gentlemen, (unknown before;) who were of the most pious and amiable character. Their conversation was sweet to my soul. They continued with me in my room during the space of two hours; then we prayed together. Soon they bid me farewell and went. *I then returned into my retirement and offered up thanks to God for such serious and solemn conversation.* I prayed with a free and thankful heart. O what a glorious time it was! I never prayed to God with so full view of God's goodness as I did then. It seemed as if God was teaching my wicked heart how to pray. I felt so easy that I could not help crying, Lord, Lord, increase my faith. I continued thus for several days, then that dark hour came on—though not very dark, for I had a little spark of light—and that spark of light was given for an answer to such secret prayer as I offered up to God in my heart. O that I might continually watch in my heart that I may not enter into temptation and snare of the devil.

"10. To-day I rejoiced greatly to hear many glorious news from almost every quarter and town on the state, that many sinners were brought to bow to Jesus, and that many were inquiring what they should do to be saved.

"19. I attended this evening a very solemn meeting as ever I attended. A sermon was preached by the Rev. Mr. Harvey from these words, 'The sacrifices of God are a broken spirit,' &c. Many appeared with a thoughtful and serious look. But O may they not be as those hearers who hear the words, and after all hide them from their hearts, as I do fear there are many.

"No doubt but many young people attend frequently such meetings, for the purpose of seeing others: their looks, dress, &c.—by these their minds are drawn away. O how many thoughtless and careless are there in the world! Sinners,

'You live devoid of peace,
'A thousand stings within your breast
'Deprive your souls of ease.'

"23. This morning my friend Thomas come to me with a sad countenance, and wished that we might pray together in our own language. I told him that I had no objection—that I would willingly do it. We then prayed to that Almighty God who was able to help us: and I believe that our prayers were graciously answered. We offered up two prayers in our tongue—the first time that we ever prayed in this manner. And the Lord was with us.

"*April I.* This evening my friend Thomas and myself conversed about what we would do first, at our return to our own country, and how we should begin to teach our poor brethren about the religion of Jesus Christ, &c. and many other kinds of conversation that we thought of. And we both thought that we must first go to the king; or else we must keep a school to educate the children and get them to have some knowledge of the Scriptures, and then we must give to them some idea of God. But these thoughts seemed to be blind on some accounts—not knowing how to do better without God's direction. *The most thought that come to my mind, was to leave all in the hand of the Almighty God; as he seeth fit.* The means may easily by done by us, and all other duties which God commands, but to make others believe in the reality of religion, no one could do it, to open blind eyes of sinners, but God only. He is able 'to bring the blind by a way that they know not, and he will lead them in paths which they have not known.'

"2. As I was just rising up this morning and looked out of my bed-room window, I saw the sun rising in the east, (Sabbath) and I wondered that my life should be kept so safely during the whole night. I thought how many unready lives were taken before the morning comes. This made my heart cry, Lord, prepare me, prepare me for death. I spent the greater part of the night in secret prayers in my bed, and found sweet communion with my God. 'Commune with your own heart upon your bed and be still.' O that the grace of God may be sufficient for me! Lord, fill my hungry soul with spiritual food.

"3.   This day I set apart for secret prayer, and the Lord was graciously with me, and has given me some spirit to pray. It seemed as if I could not enjoy myself better in any worldly conversations that I did in prayer. I can say, as I trust, that the Spirit of God has been with me this day. God appeared to be gracious and lovely. Holy thou art, O Lord God of hosts! O Lord, look down with a pitying eye upon this thy servant, whom thou hast brought from a heathen land! Be gracious to all the rest of my heathen brethren who are now in this country. Do now, O Lord hear my call. Let not the Lord remember former sins which were known to thee.

"7. This afternoon I attended the funeral of an aged person. Many people attended and many tears were shed upon almost every cheek for the loss of their friend. But, O weepers, weep for yourselves, (he was a friend of Christ it is hoped,) for he has gone in peace.

"I thought with great astonishment how little idea we have of death and eternity. Who can stop the approaching of death? May the Lord teach me to know the number of my days! O that the everlasting arm may raise my soul from deepest hell, and direct my step toward the peaceful shore of blessed eternity!

"9. To-day is my first year since I made a profession of religion. I set apart this day for prayer, and returned thanks to God for his wonderful grace and kindness towards me as a lost sinner. Though how little have I done towards him! how little have I done for his glory! Shall I live to see the end of another year? Lord, increase my faith.

"12. To-day the Lord turned me to look into my heart, to see whether there be any holiness in me. But I found nothing but 'wounds, and bruises, and putrefying sores.' I saw my sins were very great, and never were known before. I had seen my own sin before, but the Lord never show me so much, as I recollect, to make the soul sink in deep sorrow for sin, as he did this day. But it was my own blindness too. When I considered my former life, and looked into it, nothing but a heavy burden of sin was upon me. I pray the Lord that he may not remember my past sin. *O may not the God of Isaac and Jacob hide from the tears of such dying sinner as I!*

"I enjoyed myself much this day in fasting, prayer, and supplication.

"I have been thinking this day to know what is the state of man; whether they are pure from all sin: —for last evening I had a dispute with a young man. He asked me whether I do believe that we sin by words, thoughts, and deeds. I answered him yes. Certainly we do, unless we take heed to our ways—as David speaks for himself in Ps. 39. 'O mortal man,' says he, 'do we then always sin?' Yes, I answered. The Apostle speaks, 'If we say we have no sin, we deceive ourselves.' How many ways that a creature can be deceived!

"15. I attended a prayer-meeting this afternoon, and a number have been examined to be brought forward to the church. I have thought a great deal this day about my unfaithfulness and barrenness since I made a profession of religion:—how my wicked heart has turned away from God in a most evil and unkind manner. But when I considered that I sin against my Maker, I always feel sorry: and all sins which I commit raise my tears from my eyes:—as I have this afternoon been weeping very deeply because of my sins. Many times I am apt to fall into sin; but if God hears my crying for forgiveness, I shall still live devoted to him. Is there any thing that we may be cleansed by from our sins but the blood of the Lamb of God? No, in no wise.

"21. O what a solemn meeting to-day at the house of Dea. B. It was a serious and joyful time. It seemed to me that the Lord was with us. I took notice that almost every person in the room appeared very joyful. Many persons kept their heads downwards with tears on their faces. We had then neither sermon nor any discourse delivered, but many prayers were offered up for those who were rolling sin as a sweet morsel under their tongue. A number of pious men tried to speak, but they could not; for the fear of the Lord had fell upon them, that they could not; for the fear of the Lord had fell upon them, that they could not finish their discourse, but to weep. O how myself felt then. I saw that it was the Lord's work, who hath power to make sinners feel, and to show himself that he is God alone. O that the Lord may carry on his work!

"*May 5.* This day I have attended the sacrament of the Lord's supper. I felt guilty of my unfruitfulness, and had but little faith in Him whose blood is drink indeed, and whose flesh is meat indeed. I could not help weeping whilst the minister addressed those who were to be admitted into the church—warning them to be fruitful. On account of this warning I could not put a stop to my weeping eye, for I felt that I had had a stupid and cold heart, wanting of divine grace.

"8. I have been reading this morning the history of pious women, and I was very much pleased to see and to know how Christians feel. Their employment ever day was to address their heavenly Father in secret, and to read some portion of the Holy Scriptures.

"15. This day I took a walk for exercise at the distance of two or three miles. On my way home I met an aged man, unknown before, who I judged to be about sixty years of age. He was traveling on the same way that I was, and I thought in myself that I would take this opportunity to converse with him upon religious subjects: as it was my duty, (and as I have done with many other unacquainted persons before.) As we were walking, 'What bad going is this!' said he, 'I have never known such time as this.' With his observation I spoke this— 'Ought we not to be thankful to our Maker for such season as this, as well as we do for the finest weather?' 'O yes, sir I think we ought to,' says he, 'though I do not feel thankful as I ought.' With this saying, I then asked him to know whether he was one that was born again of the Holy Spirit. To which he replied, 'O I hope so; though I was one of the sheep that was almost gone, for ever lost, yet I hope that I am found.' I asked him whether he ever met with any difficulty or troubled in his mind. He answered, 'O yes, great deal; but when I meet with any trouble, I wish to be alone, and pray to God, and ask him for such comfort as I need. Before I was brought into light I thought many times that the religion of Jesus was hard thing to seek for—but it was nothing else but my own heart, I found no holiness at all but all manner of evils are lodged in it.' Soon we parted from each other, and we both wished to be remembered in our prayers.

"*June 1.* This morning I have been walking out for some secret duty. As I walked through the field alone, lo! I heard the sweet songs of many birds singing among the branches; for it was a beautiful Sabbath morning. Whilst I thus hearked, this part of a Psalm come into my soul very sweetly,

> 'Sweet is the mem'ry of thy grace,
> My God, my heavenly King;
> Let age to age thy righteousness
> In sound of glory sing,' &c.
> *Henry Obookiah*

"I thought of Christians as soon as I heard these birds tuning their joyful songs around the tree. Christians as soon as they leave their fleshly songs with their bodies in the silent tomb, will be at rest beyond all pain, death, sorrow, and trouble; and come around their King of glory, and tune their golden harps to Immanuel's praise. And then say one to another,

> 'Come let our voices join to raise
> A sacred song of solemn praise,' &c.

"16. This evening I attended some serious exercises of prayer with a few young men of pious character. Five pious young men came to our room for this purpose. They appeared to be very much engaged in the cause of the great Redeemer. We spent our time in solemn prayer for two or three hours. I found comfort myself easy in every duty which I was commanded by my God to do.

"23. I was visited this morning by a pious and good Rev. Mr. H. of L. who instructed me in a most affectionate and tender manner; and has given me some of the clearest views of Christian character, such as I needed.

"I was entreated b this friend of Christ concerning my future happiness, and was warned to live above this world, with humble and tender heart. But O, who can know my own unfruitfulness and vileness, but he who 'searcheth the heart and trieth the reins of the children of men.' I felt in my own heart that I needed the teaching of all the people of God Many times I have thought of myself being deceived, because many evil thoughts come into my mind and put me out of the right way; but in my secret prayers I have always found happy rest to my poor and immortal soul, as if I was in the right path. O that the Lord Jesus, who doth 'bring the blind by a way that they know not,' may be the director such blind as I.

"24. We have heard to-day much good news from every quarter of the country. A work of grace has been begun in many places, and there are hundreds of hopeful converts, or newly born by the influence of the Holy Spirit. O how great and how wonderful is the arm of the Lord! reaching forth his hand toward sinners, and kindly taking them in his bosom of love. But are there not many sinners yet in the fall of bitterness and in bonds of iniquity, rejecting the free offer of salvation? Are not many opposers yet set against the truth of the Gospel of Jesus Christ? O when shall these never-dying souls find rest! It is very strange to me that so many careless and stupid sinners never think or have any concern for the worth of their immortal souls. O Lord, I entreat thee to look down with compassion upon such dying sinners as are here in this land of the Gospel light! O save them, O Lord God of hosts, save them! Glorify the riches of thy free grace in making them the heirs of thy holy kingdom. O glorious Jesus, thou Son of the Most High, have mercy on the never-dying souls of men. Thou canst do the helpless sinner good; for all homage, honor, glory, and worship are due to thee, the true promised Messiah and Redeemer of the world. Thou canst work among sinners and none can hinder thee. O Lord, save us, or we perish. I am a sinner as well as others; I feel myself an unfruitful creature; and yet I choose the Lord Jesus for my everlasting portion. I have nothing of my own to recommend myself to his holy favor. All the present that I can make unto Jesus is myself. He seeks not mine, but me only.

"25. Last evening I attended a prayer-meeting, and enjoyed great comfort to my soul. I thought how Christians all agree in their feelings toward each other in a lovely manner. I once thought while we were in the room, in such a little circle, and enjoyed ourselves in conversing here in this world, how much happiness will be found at the great court of the Almighty, when all the children of God are gathered together from the east and the west, and are set down in the kingdom of heaven. What a happy time will it be for Christians!

"*July 3.* My health being weak, I set out to walk, and at the place to which I came I found a sick woman lying upon a sick bed. She had been in that case for eight years. When she heard of my being in the house, she wanted so see me. I conversed with her concerning her case; and though she was weak in her body and mind, she could answer whatever question I put to her. I asked her whether she was willing to leave this world of sin, and to be present with her lovely Jesus. She replied, 'O yes, O yes; I hope I shall reach that peaceful shore, where I shall have neither sickness nor pain, as I have now.' Before I was about to leave her she wished me to pray with her, and this was done. She took hold of my hand and begged me to remember her, thus—'O my friend, do not forget me in your prayers; and if I do not see you again in this life, I shall in better life than this.'

"17.   I have just returned from a visit to my friends. As I was walking through the woods, I came to a house which stood at some distance from the town. As soon as I was come near the house, I found an old grey-headed man, next to the road, hoeing corn. I saw he was very aged man, and I thought it was my duty to converse with him. I stood by the fence and asked him how he did. He answered, 'Well.' I asked him whether he was well within also. But he did not understand what I mean. (This old man was about ninety years of age, and had been living without hope and without God in the world.) Immediately, I went to the old man, and spoke to him in a friendly manner, thus— 'My friend,' I said to him, 'you are a stranger to me, and I unto you; and I see that your head is full of grey hairs, and no doubt your days will soon be over.' 'I know that,' said the aged man; 'so every one has got to be as I am.' 'Well,' said I, 'what do you think of the great day of judgment? are you ready for that day?' 'O, I don't know,' said he, 'I do sometimes think that I am too far off for that day.'   'Why do you not now begin to make your peace with God, before death overtake you?' said I to the old man; 'repent and believe in the Son of God.' But the old man seemed to be very careless and stupid. I talked to him, but he kept hoeing his corn; and I followed him to the end of the field, pursuing my discourse; but he seemed to be unwilling to hear me any further, and I returned thanks to the Almighty God for the opportunity which I had with this poor old man, and bid him farewell.

"*Sabbath afternoon, August 5th*. To-day I felt more anxious for prayer than I ever did. After I returned from meeting I entered in my retirement, *where I always find comfort and joy* in my secret prayer and supplication before the great Jehovah. I now wished to see my friend Thomas, who lived a mile apart from me, and I set out to go and meet together in prayer for our own good. I went and found him reading the Bible. I urged him to go up to his room with me and be there a little while; and we took a Bible and went up. We spent some time together in prayer, til the sun was down. 'O how good and pleasant it is for brethren to dwell together in unity.' We both united in prayers, two of each. We cried to God for help, in the language of good old David,

'Search us, O God, and know our hearts, try us, and know our thoughts, and see if there be any wicked way in us, and lead us in the way everlasting. 'May the Lord be pleased to lead us both in the right way, and not in the 'way that seemeth right unto a man, but the end thereof are the ways of death.' We cried to God further, that he would teach us his way, in order to walk in his truth; and to unite our hearts both to fear his holy name.

"I told my friend Thomas how I felt that day, and how much I longed to be with him together in prayer for our poor countrymen as well as for ourselves. We both wished to have our little meeting kept up until we should be separated far from each other. We wished to have no one know it, but to look to God whenever we both come together."

The Diary of Obookiah may not have been discontinued here. A considerable part of what has been transcribed was found upon detached pieces of paper; and other similar pieces may have been mislaid. The whole he had begun to copy, but had not completed it.

For this record however of his experience of Divine grace, and of his Christian faithfulness, we would not fail to express our sincerest gratitude to Almighty God. Here may be seen much of the spirit of that great pattern of missionaries—the devoted Brainerd; and while we praise the Lord that he was pleased to impart so much of his grace to his heathen youth, and dispose him to do so much for the good of others, we would implore him to incline other Christians to follow his worthy examples; and especially that his habit of conversing freely upon religious subjects, as opportunities presented, even *"with unacquainted persons"* may be imitated by all who desire the salvation of men. His letters bear the same marks of deep solicitude for the conversion and salvation of sinners.

CHAPTER VI

LETTERS—TOUR FOR MISSIONARY CAUSE

THE FOLLWING extracts are from his letters written while residing at Canaan. The first was addressed to Deacon H. of Danby, in the state of New-York; and elderly gentleman, who had taken a very deep interest in the welfare of Obookiah, and had written to him a letter of advice soon after he made a profession of religion.

"Canaan, Dec. 1815.

"My dear Friend,

"Your letter I have received, dated the tenth of September. It was with great pleasure. I shall take your advice in the all-important things which belong to me to attend to as a professor of religion. I know that the eyes of the Lord are upon me day and night, and beholding all my wicked actions and motions in every thing which I do. O that the Lord would be my help! Am I yet in the gall of bitterness and in the bonds of iniquity? I neither do justly nor love mercy as much as I ought, nor walk humbly with God.

"The work of grace in the town of S. is till going on very powerfully. By the last account which I have heard, about one hundred forty are in a hopeful state. They are now rejoicing in the hope of the glory of God. And many others are inquiring the way to Zion, crying, 'Men and brethren, what shall we do?' In this place also many are in deepest concern about their souls. O where have sinners been so long since they had discovered the name of the Savior who was crucified upon the cross, and yet they have not come to him until now? They have known their Master's will but they have not done it. They are wise to do evil, but to do good they have no knowledge. O wretched sinners, will you come to the foot of the cross at this very moment, and ask forgiveness of sins? Hark and hear the voice of him that knocketh at the door of every sinner's heart! 'Behold I stand at the door and knock.' Christ, the Savior, is knocking, saying, Open to me, my sister, my love, my dove, my undefiled, for my head is filled with dew, and my licks with the drops of the night.' I cannot help weeping. My tears are running down for joy to hear and see sinners flocking to the Almighty Jehovah. O that all sinners may come to Christ!

> 'Stop, poor sinners, stop and think,
> Before you farther go!
> Will you sport upon the brink
> Of everlasting wo?'

"O that we may stop and think where we are, and upon what ground we are standing, whether it be holy or whether it be unholy, or whether it be our duty to do the will of God or not. We now live here upon this earth, and how long we shall live we know not. Death will soon overtake us, for we are not far from it. My dear friend, I entreat you to be much engaged in prayer for thoughtless and stupid sinners in this country as well as in others.

"I would thank you to present my humble respects to all your family. I hope I shall see them, though at present unknown to each other, in the eternal world; if I do not in this present world. May God be gracious to you all. Remember me in your sweet sacrifice of prayer before our heavenly Father.

"Your affectionate friend."

To Mr. Ephraim Burge, Jun of the State of New York, he wrote as follows:

"Canaan, May 1816.

"Having received your most kind and affectionate letter a few days ago, it much satisfied me. Notwithstanding you are so far from me, yet I expect to meet you at the bar of God. O how glad I am to hear from you, Ephraim. I am glad to hear that your mind has been more engaged in regard to the subject of religion than when we lived together. If it is so, my friend, that you have such thoughts in your mind, I urge you to be careful, for it is an awful thing to be deceived. Set your heart toward Christ, and in him you may find help. Our sins are very great and reach over our heads, and there is nothing which can make them smaller or stop them but the precious blood of the Lamb of God, who has all power to take away sin from the world. The Lord Jesus expressed himself thus—'I that speak in righteousness, mighty to save.'

"You mentioned in your letter that the religion of Jesus Christ is glorious privilege. O my friend, it is so. We can say or think that his religion is a very important thing, if any one should have it, but we are not willing to seek for it. If the Lord has been pleased to operate on your mind by the influences of His Holy Spirit, as you trust he has, I hope the Lord will still continue his work in your through life. But let me entreat you to put your whole trust in God; make him sure as your own friend, and above all, give yourself entirely into the hands of your Savior, who came to seek and to save that which was lost. When you write to me, let me know all about your feelings. I long to see you, my friend, and all your father's family. I remember all your father's and mother's kindness while I was with them; though I am in fear that I do not feel thankful enough to God for it.

"If you should ever come to Connecticut, do take some pains to find me where I am, for I long to see you with brotherly love.

"I would desire your solemn prayer before your heavenly Father for

"Your affectionate friend."

TO MR. E. W. OF TORRINGFORD

August 5, 1816.

"My dear Friend,

"I hope you will not think it strange that such an one as I should write to you; for I am full of concern for the souls of others. O that the Lord would direct you in the right path. May the Lord teach me what I ought to write this day. I have heard that your sickness is still continuing. But O how is it with you now? Look now, my dear Elijah, and see whether you are prepared or unprepared, or whether you are fit to die or unfit—whether you are the Lord's or not. O my friend, consider how many are there who have been wheeled down to endless torments in the chariots of earthly pleasures, while others have been whipped to heaven by the rod of affliction. O how good had it been for some of them if they had ever known the way of life by the crucified Savior. We have great reason to tremble when the Holy Scripture teaches us that few shall be saved—much more when it tells us, that of that rank of which we are, but few shall be saved; for it is written. 'Many are called, but few chosen.' I often think of you, my dear friend Elijah, since I heard of your sickness. You perhaps sometimes think about dying—and what must be your end—and how you have misimproved your best opportunities, &c. O what a dreadful thing it is to die in a sinful state! My friend, how do you expect to find joy and peace in heaven if you should die in your sin? How have you neglected the free offer of salvation, which is offered to you 'without money and without price!' Haste, O my poor friend and get up out of your sleep of sin and death, and the Lord Jesus Christ will give you life, comfort, health and strength—for there is none but Christ can do a helpless sinner good. Now, therefore, my friend, haste to look to Christ with faith, and ask for mercy and forgiveness of your sin. I feel for you, my dear friend—for the worth of your poor and never-dying soul. O don't refuse this lovely and welcome Savior any longer:—the more you reject him, the more you grow worse; the more you hate him, the greater will be your condemnation. O poor Elijah, choose the meek and lowly Jesus for your everlasting portion. Consider the danger in which you now live upon the brink of everlasting wo. Your sickness, I fear, will take you away from the world into a solemn and silent grave. O Elijah, Elijah W. where are you? Are you willing to leave this world of sin and death and be at rest? Are you willing to die now? In time of sickness we ought to keep our hearts right towards God, in order to be cheerfully willing to die. For 'death is harmless to the people of God.'—'The righteous hath hope in his death,' but 'the wicked is driven away in his wickedness.' Follow not, my dear friend, after the example of mankind, but after Christ's—make no kind of excuse, turn unto God and live. Be not offended because I have taken this opportunity to write to you in such a manner. Let all be taken into serious consideration. It cannot hurt you, my earthly friend. And it may keep your heart from shrinking back, to consider that death is necessary to fit you for the full enjoyment of God. Whether you are willing to die or not, there certainly is no other way to complete the happiness of your soul. The happiness of the eternal world of heaven commences immediately after death. Now can you, my dear Elijah, say, 'I will arise and go to my Father, and say, Father I have sinned,' &c. O why are you so unwilling to accept the free offer of mercy? And why will you still shut Christ out of the door of your heart; when he still is knocking, and saying, 'Open to me, my sister, my love,' &c. O poor friend of mine! I do not speak of your being poor in body, but your soul is poor—wanting the bread of life. This is why I need to speak of your being poor; for without the love of God in the heart of a man, that man is poor.

"If you are a friend of Christ, be not afraid of death and eternity; for death cannot hurt you, nor your soul. Why then are you afraid that your sickness is unto death? If you were to die in sin—if death were to reign over you 'as a tyrant—to feed upon you as a lion doth upon his prey'—if death were to you to be the prison of hell, then you might reasonably startle and shrink back from it with horror and dismay. But if your sin has been blotted out of the book of God's remembrance; or if the Savior has begun his good work in you, why should you be afraid of being taken away from the world? and why not bid welcome to the king of terrors? My dear Elijah, our lives are short, and, like the smoke of the fire, are hastening away.

> 'Well, if our days must fly,
> We'll keep their end in sight.

"Remember, my dear Elijah, that I am not the teacher of the heart, nor the judge of it. The Lord Jesus is your teacher—he can make you feel. He can make the blind to see—and the lame to walk—and the sick to be healed—and above all, he can make you and I happy or miserable in eternity. All that I have said to you, my friend, will be remembered in the day of God's wrath. You and I shall both render our account to that God who has made us, at the day of judgment, for what deeds we have done in the body—whether we have done every thing right in the sight of Jehovah, or whether we have not. May the Lord God of hosts bless you. May Jesus make you faithful unto death, and that you may have at last the crown of life in the eternal world of glory.

"You, O parents of Elijah, you have the means of doing good to your own souls—to improve your time in the service of God. Where then shall you be after the returning of your bodies to the dust—when your bodies shall become food for the worms of the earth?

"Brothers and sisters of the sick man—your days will soon be over; and the road upon which you are all riding towards eternity soon will be ended. Remember. O my friends, that the eyes of the Lord are upon you all, beholding the evil and the good. Your souls are worth a thousand and million times more than such a world as this. Be careful lest they be lost in the snares and temptations of Satan, for they are many and ready to carry away your souls into darkness and despair. O that the Lord would smile upon you in pity and compassion, and save you from eternal death. Look up now, my friends, to Christ—which is your life."

The following letter was written to Mr. W. C. a member of Yale College.

"Canaan, Sept. 7, 1816.

"My dear Friend,

"Our interview yesterday was but short, and our short conversation with each other was sweet to my soul. You requested me to write to you, for which I am now taking my pen to begin our correspondence; not because I am destitute of companions here, but for our everlasting good. There is one of the best friends who is above all earthly friends, even Christ Jesus the Lord. But we are all by nature the greatest and strong enemies to him. 'All have sinned and come short of the glory of God.' We are naturally opposers to God, and to the holiness of his nature, and unable to accept of his mercy which is offered to us 'without money and without price.'

"I have reason to bless Jesus Christ, that he has wonderfully turned my feet from the path that leadeth down to endless wo. There is nothing more that I can do for him, for his great and wonderful work in the soul of such an one as I, than to be thankful for all which I now enjoy. But this is not all—'Give me thine heart, and let thine eyes observe my ways.' I hope that the God of all grace has been gracious to you, as he has to me. O that we both may rejoice with joy unspeakable and full of glory here and hereafter. The religion of Jesus which we now have embraced (as we hope we are passed from death unto life) is a strong helper to the soul, to help us on to the peaceful shore.

"I wish I could express my weak feelings to you, but alas, I cannot. It is a difficult thing to tell you that I love my Maker more than I do any thing else. Truly I do not love him enough. I have faith in him but a little—but I am sure I wish to love him more and serve him better than I now do. O what a stupid wretch and hardhearted sinner am I! Why should I have been spared so long, while many of my fellow-mortals are gone over the other side of the gloomy grave, and I am yet on this side of eternity. O where are those now who have gone before me? Remember, my dear friend, that we shall soon return to the dust, and leave this world of perplexity and trouble, and all the useless pleasures in it, and be fore ever miserable or happy in the presence of the King of glory. O how happy it will be for Christian souls to meet together and uniting their hearts in love at that time.

> 'When shall I reach that happy place,
> And be for ever blest?
> When shall I see my Father's face,
> And in his bosom rest?'

"It is no matter how long or short the lives of Christians are, if their best moments are well improved, in order to meet their lovely Jesus in peace whenever they are called for. Let us live, my dear friend, as strangers and pilgrims on earth—let us feel lively in the faith of the Son of God—let us both seek for a better country than this—let us be faithful and humble believers of Jesus. I think I can truly say to my Lord, Lord, my body and soul are in thine hands, do with them according to thy holy will. Thy will be done, and not mine. The happiness of this world is nothing but a dream. It will soon pass away as the wind that bloweth. We must give up all for heaven, lest we perish at the presence of the Judge. The best present that we ought to make to Christ, is to give our whole hearts to him—and not 'gold and frankincense and myrrh,' as wise men of the East did.

"Do remember, my friend, those that are around you whose sins are unpardoned. Do pray for them. Remember my poor countrymen, who know not the way of life by a Redeemer. Do not forget to pray for your affectionate friend,

"HENRY OBOOKIAH."

Toward the close of the year 1816 Henry went to Amherst, Massachusetts, for the purpose of accompanying the Rev. Mr. Perkins, an agent of the Board of Commissioners for Foreign Missions, in a tour through that section of the country, to solicit donations for the benefit of the Foreign Mission School. The success of the solicitations was greatly promoted by the presence of Obookiah. Contributions were highly liberal, and often drawn from sources not before accustomed to yield any aid to purposes of charity.

The interest which he had excited towards himself personally is expressed in a letter from Rev. Mr. Perkins, written soon after his death. "He was much beloved," he says, "by all who knew him in this region. He had awakened a lively interest in his welfare among them;

and his death has cast a gloom over them which will not soon be dispelled. His recall to the world of spirits is one of those deep things of Providence which we cannot fathom."

A letter since received from the same respected source, contains several facts and observations which illustrate his character and evince the peculiar acceptableness and influence of his visit in that quarter.

"I have rarely, if ever," says Mr. Perkins, "seen a person who seemed to set so high a value on time as Obookiah. What others would call leisure hours, would be busy hours with him. When alone, he was diligent in his literary studies. When in company, improvement was his object—and if the conversation was not immediately interesting to him, he would take his Pocket Testament and read, or repair to his study and his books.

"At a little circle of friends one evening, he said to me in a whisper, 'Time is precious, here are a few souls going to eternity, 'tis a good opportunity to improve.' Just as we were about to retire at the close of the evening, he addressed two youth in the room for a few minutes on the subject of religion, with great apparent effect. Whether the alarm of conscience, which he was instrumental of exciting, proved lasting or not, I have never known. So valuable was time in his estimation that if he had passed a day or an hour unprofitably, he would speak of it with deep regret.

"His humility deserves our notice. In visiting different towns, it was my practice to gratify the people by calling on Obookiah to address them on the subject of Christianity. He was always appropriate, solemn, and interesting. Many flattering remarks were frequently made to him on that account. But though this was calculated to foster pride and inspire him with unbecoming confidence, yet it actually produced the opposite—humility and self-distrust. A circumstance took place which justifies this observation.

"At a village of considerable magnitude, after the missionary service had been performed, the pastor of the church appointed an evening meeting. Just before the meeting, it was observed to Obookiah that some remarks would be expected from him. He modestly declined. The subject was urged. He said, 'I'm a poor heathen, I don't know enough to teach people who live in Christian land.' Being under my care, he applied to me to excuse him from the service. I replied to him, that I believed it to be his duty. The people had contributed generously. They were anxious to hear him speak on the subject of religion. You have always succeeded well; and what you shall say may prove a savor of life to some soul. Some after, as we were passing to the meeting house, observing his extreme reluctance, I asked the Rev. Mr. B. to urge and encourage him. Many things were said to persuade him, but his reluctance appeared to be invincible. As we arrived at the door, he again fled to me for refuge. Said he, 'Do excuse me—I can't say any thing. You can preach—it will do more good.' I told him I could not, as the people would be greatly disappointed. But when I said this, such had been his anxiety, and such his manner of expressing his feelings, that tears instantly started in his eyes, and gladly would I have preached for his relief. When the proper time came, he was called upon to address the meeting. He deliberately rose and addressed the people with his usual propriety and seriousness. At the close of the service I passed by his pew and invited him to walk with me. He was bathed in tears. I did not hesitate about the cause. I tried much to soothe his feelings, but it was to no purpose. Mr. B. perceiving them, made an attempt to pacify him, but was unsuccessful; his soul seemed to refuse comfort. This was on our way to our lodgings. When we arrived at the house, I mentioned his feelings to the kind family where we were to lodge. Every expedient was tried to restore him to his wonted cheerfulness; but all our efforts were unavailing. After about an hour, one of the family took a seat near him, with a view to divert his mind. This attempt was successful—and the first sentence he uttered was, 'I'm a poor unworthy sinner—I feel as though I was lost.' His customary cheerfulness soon returned, and many in the little circle, who sat a long time sorrowing had their sorrow turned into joy.

"The Bible was his best and constant companion. He always carried in his pocket a Testament, which was presented to him by a friend who is now a missionary to the heathen. At a certain time he went about 10 miles to visit one of his countrymen. In changing his clothes, he left his Pocket Testament. On his return, he pleasantly said to me, 'Blind man don't walk very safely without his staff.'

"Obookiah's visit to this part of the country was of essential service to the cause of Foreign Missions. It has silenced the weak but common objection against attempting to enlighten the heathen, that they are too ignorant to be taught. This sentiment has prevented much exertion. It had a wicked origin. We have first enslaved our fellowbeings, then degraded them by every menial service, deprived them of the means of mental improvement, and almost of human intercourse; and because, under this circumstances, people of color are devoid of knowledge, we have hastened to the irrational conclusion that all the heathen are a race of idiots. Adopting this conclusion, multitudes are utterly opposed to making any attempt to turn them from darkness to light. Influenced by this opinion, groundless as it is, no reasonings, or arguments, or motives which can be offered, are of any avail. But the appearance of Obookiah has done much in this region to wipe off this disgrace thrown upon the heathen, and to remove the objection so often made. The proof he gave of talents as well as of piety, carried conviction to many that the heathen had souls as well as we, and were as capable of being enlightened and Christianized. Acknowledgements to this effect have frequently been made to me; and now in the circle of *his* travels, there is no occasion to combat this objection.

"Another effect produced by his visit to this region is, that it has roused the slumbering energies of those who have hitherto done nothing in the Missionary cause. Many have become interested for the benighted heathen, and satisfied that the conversion of them to Christianity is practicable. And though they have never before lifted a finger or contributed a mite, have now been prevailed on to do something. In several instances dollars were handed me by persons who confessed that they had never done any thing before. This is an effect produced which probably will not be transient, but permanent. A feeling in the cause of Missions has been excited which will not soon subside.

"His visit has moreover enkindled a spirit of prayer and benevolence in the bosoms of God's children, which was very much needed. Coldness and a circumscribed charity were too apparent. Especially were these visible with respect to the heathen. But now there is evidently an increase of fervency and holy wrestling in the addresses of Christians to the throne of grace. They intercede for the unevangelized nations as though it was their hearts' desire that they might be saved. Their benevolent efforts are more numerous and more liberal. They not only exert *themselves* in this glorious cause, but they use their influence to induce *others* to come and do likewise. They refer them to Obookiah as an instance of the propriety and practicability of missionary exertion. While this instance encourages their own efforts, it greatly emboldens them in urging upon others the necessity and expediency of constant exertion in the cause of the heathen.

"Such have been the effects of Obookiah's tour in this region. And since such are the effects, and such was his character, it is not surprising that his death is so much lamented. Many flattering hopes were excited in the breasts of his friends here. A righteous Providence has seen fit to blast them. But we have a foundation for our hopes that cannot be shaken. On this we may rest the heathen cause and feel secure, while human means and promising agents are swept away."

The following letter was written by Obookiah, while at Amherst, to his companions at South Farms in Litchfield.

"Amherst, Jan. 1, 1817.

"My dear Brethren,

"I long to see you all. You may perhaps be glad to hear from me, and to know how I am. I hope you are doing well, both in your studies and your religious exercises of the morning and the evening, which is the duty of prayer.

"I have seen one of our own countrymen at Enfield, about nine miles from this place. He has been in that place for ten years, and two years at Boston. Thus he continued in this country just twelve years. He came from Hawaii, and his native place was Koihi, (well known such place.) From that place Capt. John took him on board the ship, and brought him over here, when he was not but fourteen years of age. His native name was Nahlemah-hownah. Since I saw him I could converse with him but little, for he has lost the greatest part of our language; but he could recollect the names of many things, as far as he was able to describe them to me. While I was with him he could not keep away his eyes from me, for wonder and gladness to see such an one who came from his own country. I staid with him two days at Enfield not long since. I spent the whole of my time with him while I was there. The first that I did, I took him by my side, to converse with him upon the serious subjects. By his own words I judged him to be as the one who was willing to accept of the free offer of mercy, though I fear he may in a time of temptation fall away, and all that which is sown in the heart. O my dear brethren and friends, he needs your prayers! Pray for him, that he may be brought to see the goodness of the Lord, and that he may be faithful to his own soul. Do not delay your prayers to the Almighty God for such an one that is very dear to you. He now feels as though he was one of the greatest sinners that ever lived. Do you not all feel anxious for the soul of your own countryman here now in this county? O that he may devote himself to the service of his Creator! I observed many times while I prayed with him, he would deeply cry, with such a dismal gloom as if the wrath of the Almighty was upon him. I have heard last Sabbath noon, by a man who was well known to him, that this young man becomes more thoughtful ever since I come away. If this be the case, I would humbly beg at the mercy-seat for your prayers, that they may not be hindered. I shall see him again before a long time. He longs to see you.

"May God be with you all."

The youth here mentioned was afterwards a member of the Foreign Mission School, and exhibited hopeful evidence of piety. The impressions made by the conversation of Obookiah were never lost. His English name is George Sandwich.

CHAPTER VII

CONNECTION WITH FOREIGN MISSION SCHOOL— CHARACTER—SICKNESS—DEATH

HENRY RETURNED from Amherst, in April, to South Farms. Here he remained with his countrymen until the first of May, when the Foreign Mission School was removed to Cornwall.

He now had his mind bent upon becoming prepared, as soon as practicable, to preach the Gospel. He paid particular attention to preaching, and made many remarks upon the subjects of sermons and the manner of delivering them.

Some observations upon a common defect in preaching are well recollected. He complained of the practice of those ministers who used such language in their sermons as was unintelligible to most of their hearers. Ministers, he said, preached to persons of every description; almost all were ignorant, *very few* had learning, and if they preach to *all* the people, they ought to use plain language. If not, he said, "as well might preach in unknown tongue." *Every word,* he thought, should be plain, for "people," said hem "can't carry *dictionary to meeting.*"

As Obookiah, at the time of his entrance into the school at Cornwall, had arrived at an age of considerable maturity, it may be proper that a more particular description should now be given of his person and character.

He was considerably above the ordinary size; but little less than six feet in height, and in his limbs and body proportionably large. His form, which at sixteen was awkward and unshapen, had become erect, graceful, and dignified. His countenance had lost every mark of dullness; and was, in an unusual degree, sprightly and intelligent. His features were strongly marked. They were expressive of a sound and penetrating mind. He had a piercing eye, a prominent Roman nose, and a chin considerably projected.

His complexion was olive, differing equally from the blackness of the African and the redness of the Indian. His hair was black, worn short, and dressed after the manner of the Americans.

In his *disposition* he was amiable and affectionate. His temper was mild. Passion was not easily excited, nor long retained. Revenge, or resentment, it is presumed, was never known to be cherished in his heart.

He loved his friends, and was grateful for the favors which he received from them. In his journal and letters are found frequent expressions of affection and gratitude to those how had been his benefactors. To families in which he had lived, or to individuals who had been his particular patrons, he felt an ardent attachment. One of the latter, his early friend at New-Haven, who had been separated from him for a considerable time, he met with great delight; and after the first customary salutations, said to him, "I want to see you great while: you don't know how you seem to me: you seem like *father, mother, brother, all.*"

In his understanding, Obookiah excelled ordinary young men. His mind was not of a common cast. It was such that, with proper culture, it might have become a mind of the first order. Its distinguishing traits were sound common sense, keen discernment, and an inquisitiveness or enterprise which disposed him to look as far as his mind could reach into every subject that was presented to his attention.

By his good sense he was accustomed to view subjects of every kind in their proper light; to see things as they are. He seldom misconceived or misjudged. By his companions his counsel was sought, and regarded as decisive. He had that clear sense of propriety, with regard to his own conduct and the conduct of others, which always commands the respect excites the fear of those who behold it. Had he been disposed to cultivate a talent for this purpose, he would have become one of the severest of critics upon the manners and conduct of those around him.

Few persons have a deeper insight into the characters of men, or have the power of forming a more just estimate of them, by their words and actions, than he had. Few are more capable of perceiving the exact import of *language,* or are less liable to be deceived, as to its real meaning, by a designed ambiguity of terms.

His inquisitiveness existed in relation to all subjects of interest, and disposed him to make himself acquainted with every thing that was known by others, and to discover whatever was within his reach.

His inquisitive mind was not satisfied with pursuing the usual round of study, but he was disposed to understand critically every branch of knowledge to which he attended. For this reason his progress in his studies was not rapid—but, as a scholar, he was industrious, ingenious, and thorough. His mind was also inventive. After having acquired some slight knowledge of the English language in its grammatical construction, he entered upon the project of reducing to system his own native tongue. As it was not a written language, but lay in its chaotic state, everything was to be done. With some assistance he had made considerable progress towards completing a Grammar, a Dictionary, and a Spelling-book.

He had also translated into his native tongue the whole of the Book of Genesis.

These specimens of his industry and ingenuity, when seen, administer severe reproof to the sloth and dullness of most persons of much greater age and of advantages far superior to his own.

When Obookiah became a member of the Foreign Missions School, he had attended to all the common branches of English education. In reading, writing, and spelling, he was perhaps as perfect as most young men of our own country, of the same age and with common opportunities. He wrote a legible manly hand, and had acquired the habit of writing with considerable rapidity. He had at this time studied the English Grammar so far as to be able to phrase most sentences with readiness. He understood the important rules in common Arithmetic, and had obtained considerable knowledge of Geography. He had studied also one book of Euclid's Elements of Geometry, and of his own accord, without a regular instructor, had acquired such knowledge of the Hebrew, that he had been able to read several chapters in the Hebrew Bible, and had translated a few passages in to his native language. He had a peculiar relish for the Hebrew language, and from its resemblance to his own, acquired it with great facility; and found it much less difficult to translate than the English into his native tongue.

The winter before he came to the school he commenced the study of Latin. This he pursued principally after he became a member of the Institution.

In his *manners,* Obookiah was habitually grave and reserved. In the presence of his friends, however, his conversation was often sprightly, and rendered particularly entertaining by a fondness for humor, for which he was distinguished. This he oftener exhibited by a quick perception and relish of it in others, than by actually displaying it in himself. Yet he sometimes gave evidence in his own remarks of possessing no small degree of genuine wit. When conversing with his companions in their native language, he frequently afforded them much amusement by the pleasant and humorous cast of his conversation.

The customary deportment of Obookiah, however, was serious, and dignity strikingly characterized his manners. Few young men, it is presumed, command so much respect from persons of every age and character. Notwithstanding the familiarity which he used with his companions, he maintained an influence over them becoming the relation of an elder brother, or even that of a respected parent. In his intercourse with *them* the dignity of his character was peculiarly visible. A motion of his head often made known to them his will, and obtained the compliance which he desired.

His manners had become in a considerable degree refined. A gentleman of respectability who visited Cornwall, and had a particular interview with him, observed that he had met with but few persons of any country more gentlemanly in their manners, or intelligent and interesting in their conversation.

Obookiah was a decided and consistent *Christian*. His conduct was habitually under the influence of principles of piety. He manifested a strong interest in the general prosperity of religion, and expressed, in his conversation as well as his letters and diary, ardent desires for the salvation of his fellow-men; and especially of his *countrymen*, for whom he fervently prayed, and in whose behalf he often requested the earnest prayers of his friends.

In his writings satisfactory evidence is furnished of his own personal experience of the power of divine grace. In these may be seen his convictions concerning the character of his unrenewed heart; his views of the grace and glory of the Savior; his entire reliance upon the merits of Christ for justification, and the employments and duties in which he found his only happiness through the whole course of his Christian life.

Besides this evidence, and that which was furnished by his exemplary conduct, the following facts will afford additional proof of his ardent piety.

While a member of the Institution at Cornwall, he was in the habit of attending a weekly meeting with his companions on Saturday evening; in which, in addition to the usual exercises of a religious meeting, he questioned them individually concerning the state of their minds, and addressed to them such observations as the particular situation of each seemed to demand. Others in a few instances have been present, and have been greatly surprised both at the ability which he possessed of eliciting the feelings of his companions, and at the pertinency and wisdom of his remarks.

He once observed to a friend, whilst in health, "I have *many times* so much enjoyment in the night, I cannot sleep."

At another time, "*When I have done wrong I am always sorry—I am so sorry!*"

He excelled and delighted in prayer. In a letter from the Rev. Mr. Perkins, who often witnessed his performance of this duty in public assemblies, and had also a favorable opportunity of becoming acquainted with his secret devotions, it is observed, "Prayer seemed to be his daily and nightly business. In this duty he not only appeared to take great delight, but he was pertinent, copious, and fervent. It was almost impossible to hear him pray and not be drawn into a devotional frame. I have repeatedly witnessed great numbers in a meeting melted into weeping, and in one instance the greater part of the assembly, and several sobbing, while he stood before the throne of God, filling his mouth with arguments and pleading for christian and heathen nations.

"He remarked to me one morning as we were journeying, that the night previous he had spent chiefly in prayer for a youth who resided in the family where we had been kindly entertained."

He was once requested by a clergyman to attend a religious meeting with him, and make such observations as he thought proper to the people. Previously to the hour appointed for the meeting he proposed to the minister that they should retire and spend a short time in supplicating the blessing of God upon the duties they were about to perform.

Obookiah considered it his duty, and made it his habitual practice to converse as he had opportunity, with persons whom he supposed to be destitute of grace, and urge upon them the necessity of immediate repentance. In several instances his conversation has made impressions which have terminated in an apparent conversion of the soul to God.

After Henry's return from Massachusetts, he maintained correspondence with several persons of respectability residing in the different parts of the country which he had visited. A very few only of his letters have been obtained; and parts of these are of so local and private a nature as to prevent their being inserted with propriety in this volume.

Extracts from two of them will follow. The first was addressed to S. W. Esq. of Greenfield, Massachusetts.

"Cornwall, June 16, 1817.

"My dear Sir,

"Again I take my pen to embrace this opportunity in writing. Indeed, on this very day I received a most affectionate letter; and when I came to unseal it, lo! it was from my dear beloved friend Mr. S. W.! How, or what answer can I give for it? My dear friend, I received your letter with a thankful heart. I rejoice to hear that you have still a lively thought concerning the great things of eternity. O that our thoughts and hearts may be united together in the fear of God, and in love of the Lord Jesus—whom you spoke well of. Indeed, my dearest friend, we are in a great debt, both to God and to his Son Jesus Christ. We owe them ten thousands of talents! and alas! how would we repay for all? Notwithstanding the greatness of our due to God, for all his goodness and kindness towards us, yet we can repay it, by giving up ourselves to him; for he does not with for ours, but us—for thus it is written, 'My son, give me thine heart, and let thine eyes observe my ways.' Your observations which you made in this your letter, are just as the thoughts of a true and humble believer in God—and as one that fears God. Surely it is as you say, that the supreme love and affection must we give to him, who is the Lord over all, and blessed forever. Pray that these thoughts may not be mislaid in our hearts.

"Since I received your letter, my companions had the curiosity to know the person from whom the letter was sent. I told them from one of my friends at the place where I was kindly treated. They were very much pleased with the letter—supposed that you was a friend of Christ, and a true believer in God, by what you spoke, both of Christ and his character. To whom I answered that I had a strong love for you, and hope that you may be a fellow-traveler through the journey of this wilderness. O that we both may meet in the presence of God in the eternal world above—where sin will never enter. Let us not neglect the duty which we owe to God to love him with our hearts, souls, and strength—and let us *pray without ceasing.*

"With this I must leave you, my dear friend, in the hand of God. Look to him to receive instruction and to know his holy character."

The following letter was written to A. S. Esq. of Amherst, dated

"Cornwall, August 15, 1817.

"My dear Friend,

"Your letter of late gave me great satisfaction; and since I have received it I do now think that I was in fault for not giving you an answer for it sooner; but be so kind as excuse me. You know now what joy and pleasure I have had since I received your letter. O what happy news! It gives me great joy to hear that the Lord has visited Amherst once more with the influences of his Holy Spirit, and that he has already plucked as brands from the burning some of those who once had been destitute of the grace of God, and are now bowing down to the scepter of King Jesus. O that the professed followers of the meek and lowly Jesus may be more and more lively in this most glorious work of our blessed Redeemer. Let every Christian be more and more deeply sensible that the glory of every good work here below must come from God; as we read that he is *the Giver of every good gift, and every perfect gift is from above.* We cannot expect to see a single soul coming out of the kingdom of Satan into the kingdom of Christ, unless we see one or more faithful and humble Christians running forward in spirit without any doubt, and failing not to do whatever duty God requires of them. O let us all entreat of the Lord that he would show unto us of his holy character and perfections, that we may be able to love and to serve him more and far better than we now do. Let us have a more realizing sense of our ingratitude and unfruitfulness in the eye of the all-seeing God; let us be faithful in our duty, and may the great grace of God be sufficient for us all.

"I have not heard any news since I came away from Amherst. The only information that I can give is the present situation of this Institution under which we are placed. Our school is going on very regularly, and the scholars are making some progress in their studies. One of our members is become new born in Christ since he has been here, and I trust there is no small degree of happiness. He is now rejoicing it he hope of the glory of God. O that the Lord would be pleased to bless this school. I humbly beg your prayers for this school, that each member of it may become a member of the household of God. Please remember me to Mr. and Mrs. P. and family. Tell Mr. P. that I shall write to ho, as soon as I can, but dare not make any promise, or set a time when.

Yours, H. OBOOKIAH."

About the commencement of the year 1818, Obookiah became seriously indisposed, and was obliged wholly to abandon his studies. A physician was called and speedy attention paid to his complaints. It was soon found that his disease was the typhus fever; and a thorough course of medicine was commenced, which after one or two weeks appeared to check the progress of the disorder, and confident expectations were entertained of his recovery. Hope continued to be cherished until it became evident that his strength was wasting, and that his constitution, naturally strong, was giving way to the violence of the disease, which had taken fast hold of him, and had not been essentially removed. Notwithstanding the unremitted care and the skill of his attending physician, (Dr. Calhoun,) and the counsel of others called to consult with him, the kindest and most judicious attentions of the family into which he had fallen, and the universal solicitude of his surrounding friends, he continued to decline until the night of the 17th of February, when his happy spirit was released, and his joyful anticipations realized, that *he should soon reach his Heavenly Father's house.*

He was confined during his sickness, and came to his peaceful end in the family of Rev. Timothy Stone, then the minister of the South Parish in Cornwall. To the kindness, Christian counsels, and good examples of this family, Obookiah and his associates were greatly indebted. The writer of the little memoir has not ceased to remember now, at the date of the edition, and he trusts will not , to the end of life, the uniform interest manifested by this family in the Foreign Mission School; and their great kindness, especially in sickness, to him and his pupils.

In this lasting lingering sickness, the Christian character of Obookiah was advantageously exhibited. His patience, cheerfulness, resignation to the will of God, gratitude for the kindness of his friends, and benevolence, were particular subjects of notice and conversation to those who attended him during this interesting period. His physician said of him that "he was the first patient whom he had ever attended through a long course of fever, that had not in some instances manifested a greater or less degree of peevishness and impatience."

Mrs. Stone, who devoted her attention exclusively to the care of the beloved youth, while his flesh and strength were wasting under the violence of this disease, observed that "this had been one of the happiest and most profitable periods of her life—that she had been more than rewarded for her cares and watchings by day and night, in being permitted to witness his excellent example, and to hear his godly conversation."

By this friend a part of his observations and answers, particularly within a few of the last days of his sickness, were committed to writing, and are as follows:

To one of his countrymen, as he entered the room in the morning, after he had passed a night of suffering, he said, "I almost died last night. It is a good thing to be sick, Sandwich—we must all die—and 'tis no matter where we are." Being asked by another, "Are you afraid to die? he answered, *"No, I am not."* A friend said to him, "I am sorry to find you so very sick"—he replied, *"Let God do as he pleases."*

Mrs. Stone frequently inquired of him if he would hear a few verses in the Bible; *"O yes!"* was his answer, *"tis good."*—and after hearing, he would turn his eyes to heaven, apparently in prayer. After a season of great distress, he broke out in an audible voice and said, "If we put our trust in God, we need not fear." Frequently, when free from pain, he inquired for some one to pray with him; but often before he could be gratified his pains returned, and he forgot his request. The person whom he most frequently called upon for this purpose was his friend Thomas. They often prayed together, alone:—as they had done for years. In the language of his female friend, "Their souls appeared to be knit together like those of David and Jonathan. Henry always appeared composed and apparently very happy after a season of prayer with Thomas. In a season of fainting I left the room for a moment to get some water, returned and found them weeping in great distress, supposing the time of separation had now come." Upon his inquiring for the doctor , to who he appeared greatly attached, Mrs. Stone said to him, "Henry, do you depend on your physician?" "Oh! You don't know," said he, "how much I depend on the great physician of the soul." He inquired, "Does the doctor say I shall get well?" It was answered, "He thinks it is uncertain,"—to which he said, "God will take care of me." He observed to Mrs. Stone, "It is a fine pleasant morning." She said to him, "You are glad to see the light of the morning, after a dark distressing night." He replied, *"Oh, some light in the night—some light of God."*

"After a season of distress for two hours, he appeared perfectly happy—he looked out of the window—his eyes appeared fixed on some delightful object. I inquired of him, "Of what are you thinking, Henry?" *"Oh! I can't tell you all,"* said he, — *"Of Jesus Christ."*

After sleeping for some time, he prayed very fervently, in these words, "O Lord, have mercy on my soul—Thou knowest all my secret sins—Save me for the sake of Jesus Christ our Lord and Savior—Amen."

He said to one of his countrymen, who had been a faithful nurse to him, "I must eat or I can't live,"—and then inquired of him with anxiety, "Have you eat breakfast, William? How thankful you ought to be that you have strength, and can eat!" Soon he raised his hands and said, *"Oh! I want to see Hawaii! But I think I never shall—God will do right—he knows what is best"*—and burst into a flood of tears. "William, if you live to go home, remember me to my uncle.

To dear H. he said, "I am thinking most of the time how good God is—how kind to me." His companions were mentioned. He said, "They are all very good; they have done a great deal for me. But they must be good for themselves to."

"He appeared very affectionate to all, especially his countrymen. He insisted on some one of them being with him continually; would call very earnestly for them if they were out of his sight; and would be satisfied with only this, that they were gone to eat or rest." To one of them he said, "W_____, I thank you for all you have done for me; you have done a great deal; but you will not have to wait on me much more—I shall not live." To another, "My dear friend S_____, you have been very kind to me; I think of you often; I thank you; but I must die, G_____, and so must you. Think of God, _____, never fail." To another, "You must stay; perhaps I finish off this forenoon. How much God has done for me and for you!"

The day before he died, "after a distressing night and a bewildered state of mind, he appeared to have his reason perfectly, and requested that his countrymen might be called." After they came in he inquired several times for one of them who was absent, and for whom he had no hope; and said, "I have not seen him much—I shan't see him—I want to talk to him." When the rest had seated themselves around his bed, he addressed them most feelingly in his native language, as long as his strength would permit. As much of the address as could be recollected was afterwards written in English by one of his countrymen; and was essentially as follows:

"My dear countrymen, I wish to say something to you all—you have been very kind to me—I feel my obligation to you—I thank you. And now, my dear friends, I must beseech you to remember that you will follow me. Above all things, make your peace with God—you must make Christ your friend—you are in a strange land—you have no father –no mother to take care of you when you are sick—but God will be your friend if you put your trust in him—he has raised up friends here for you and for me—I have strong faith in God—I am willing to die when the voice of my Savior call me hence—I am willing, if God design to take me. But I cannot leave you without calling upon the mercy of God to sanctify your souls and fit you for heaven. When we meet there we shall part no more. Remember, my friends, that you are poor—it is by the mercy of God that you have comfortable clothes, and that you are so kindly supported. You must love God—I want to have you make your peace with God. Can't you see how good God is to you? God has done great deal for you and for me. Remember that you must love God, or else you perish for ever. God has given his Son to die for you—I want to have you love God very much. I want to talk with you by and by—my strength fails—I can't now—I want to say more" _____

This was probably but a part of what was spoken, and that imperfectly translated. The address, under the circumstances in which it was made, was affecting beyond description. The weakness of Obookiah, which was such that it was with difficulty that he could utter an audible sound; the peculiarly affectionate and earnest tones of his voice,, faltering in death—his companions sitting around him with broken hearts—some of them almost unable to support their grief— the address being continued until his strength was entirely exhausted— rendered the scene literally overwhelming—loud sobbing was heard throughout the room; and from persons little accustomed to weep.

After Henry had ceased to speak, one of his countrymen, at his request, communicated in English to those of his companions who were not able to understand the Hawaiian language, such things as Henry had previously committed to him for that purpose.

An hour or two after this, when Obookiah had obtained a little rest, his countryman George Tamoree, who had been absent during the address, coming in, he said to him, "Sit down, George, I have been talking with the other boys. They have been very kind to me—I can't pay them—but the Lord Jesus has enough and to spare—not money nor wine—he will reward them. You, George, as well as I, are a poor boy—you have no father or mother here—God has given us good friends, and you must love him and serve him, George; and when we have departed here we may praise God for ever. We must all die.

Doctor C. cannot save us when we are sick unto death. You and I are sinners. May the Lord Jesus have mercy on our poor souls. I must rest."

To a son of Rev. Mr. Stone, who came to his bedside, and after looking at him, was about to withdraw, he said, "Wait—wait—I wish to speak to you. R_____, you have become a great boy—you have been to school a great deal. Remember you will be examined at the day of judgment for your improvement."

To a friend he said, "My faith hold out." To another, "How soon shall I be taken away?" It was answered, "Pretty soon." He was asked, "If you could have your choice, would you choose to live or die?" He replied, "I do not know; I wish to live to do good; if it were not for this, I do now wish to live another moment." And added, with much apparent grief, *"I've lost my time—I've lost my time."*

To another friend he said, *"I have no desire to live, if I can enjoy the presence of God, and go where Christ is."*

Looking down at his feet, which bore evident marks of approaching death, he cried out, *"Oh, mortality!"*

His physician requested him to take some medicine which was disagreeable to him; he said, "Wait, wait, sir, till tomorrow;" but soon consented, and said, "perhaps there will be no to-morrow." The evening before his death the Rev. Mr. Mills, whom he always called "Father Mills," came in to see him. He looked at him very wishfully, and said, "Will you pray, sir, before we part? He listened to the prayer with fixed attention, and when it was closed, said, as he had done in every instance before, *"I thank you, sir"*—and this with a sweetness of voice and an expression of countenance which none can conceive but those who witnessed them.

As death seemed to approach, Mrs. Stone said to him, "Henry, do you think you are dying?" He answered, "Yes, ma'am"—and then said, "Mrs. Stone, *I thank you for your kindness."* She said, "I wish we might meet hereafter." He replied, "I hope we shall."—and taking her hand, affectionately bade her *farewell.* Another friend taking his hand, told him that he "must die soon." He heard it without emotion, and with a heavenly smile bade him his last adieu.

He shook hands with all his companions present, and with perfect composure addressed to them the parting salutation of his native language, "Alloah o'e."—*My love be with you.*

But a few minutes before he breathed his last, his physician said to him, "How do you feel now, Henry?" He answered, *"Very well—I am*

not sick—I have no pain—I feel well." The expression of his countenance was that of perfect peace. He now seemed a little revived, and lay in a composed and quiet state for several minutes. Most of those who were present, not apprehending an immediate change, had seated themselves by the fire. No alarm was given, until one of his countrymen, who was standing by his bed-side, exclaimed, *"Obookiah's gone."*
All sprang to the bed. The spirit had departed—but a smile, such as none present had ever beheld—an expression of the final triumph of his soul, remained upon his countenance.

Thus lived and thus died Henry Obookiah, a more lovely and interesting youth than the most faithful memoir can describe. How great the debt to the grace of God for his conversion, and the immense benefits that have resulted from it to himself, to *his* country, and to our own. A happy spirit doubtless has he been before the throne of God, the first fruits unto Christ from his native islands; but followed since by many more who, like the excellent Kaahumanu and Keopualini survived him long enough to receive the glad tidings of salvation which he had hoped to convey to them, and joyfully to embrace the Savior— to bless God for sending them Missionaries—to recommend Christ to their dying countrymen, and then they departed to join the sainted spirit of Henry in "his Heavenly Father's house."
Let the mercy be adored that so often preserved this pioneer of salvation to his country from an untimely end. See that mercy displayed when he was bearing away his little brother from the murderous scene at the death of his parents. The arrow pierced the heart of the infant, and left the vigorous youth to escape, to tell to Christians the story of his country's sufferings and wants. The parents were too old, and the infant too young, to become, like Henry, the promising subject of grace, and accomplish all that was affected by him.
See that mercy again exhibited when about to cast himself from the fatal precipice. An orphan boy, in despair of seeing *any more good*, he was about to put an end to his life when the silent voice of God whispered to the enemy to pursue him, and rescue him again from a violent death.
Thus preserved, he sought another and, where he might be happier than to remain there "without father or mother." Passing by countries of idolatry and superstition, he was directed to a land of Christians. Here, through the goodness of God, he found *fathers* and *mothers, sisters* and *brothers*. And to crown all of his mercies, he obtained the knowledge of the true God: *"the God of Isaac and Jacob,"* as he said, *"who*

would not hide from the tears of such a dying sinner as he." He found a Savior; and joyfully devoted his life to his service, in the hope of being permitted to proclaim his love to his country and kindred.

His life was short, but it had answered, "life's great end," to himself, and had been blessed to the good of many others.

When he died, the friends of Henry mourned that such bright hopes were so soon extinguished, and that he had not lived to accomplish all that he wished for his native islands.

But, as is often true under God's good providence, he effected more by his death, doubtless, in advancing his favorite object, than he could have done in a long life. Missionaries immediately prepared to go forth, and continued to multiply upon those islands until, in less than twenty years, twenty-four Missionaries and forty-two assistants were preaching the Gospel and laboring to promote it, where, then, the glad tidings had never been heard.

The providence of God was peculiar in the introduction of Christianity there. While the first mission family was on its way, by an act of the government the system of idolatry was abolished, their idols carried away, and an effectual door opened to the Missionaries of the cross. Now missionary stations are found on nearly all that interesting group of islands. Houses of worship are built, and crowded with numerous attendants; and churches are formed, embracing hundreds of native members. Schools are established on most of the islands, and thousands of children gathered into Sabbath schools and Bible classes. The Scriptures are translated into the native language; school books, Tracts, and other works prepared; and presses established, and in active operation. A newspaper, *The Hawaiian Teacher*, is issued, and a high school, formed of members from the different islands, for the purpose of educating "native teachers and preachers of the Gospel both for the nation and other Polynesian tribes." Thus, by the divine blessing, will thousands of other minds, like that of Henry, be redeemed form darkness, ignorance, and sin; and made partakers of the light and blessings of the Gospel of Christ.

It was the exclamation of some who have been already illuminated and saved—"O that the Missionaries had come sooner to the islands! Then would our fathers and mothers have known the Savior that we know—they would have had hope in death, as we have—and we should have gone to heaven together."

Let there be many who shall respond to the call for more laborers— *"Here are we, send us;"* and let the churches be ready to forward all who will go; and are demanded; and soon we shall be prepared to unite in chanting the delightful hymn sung at the departure of the second band of Missionaries to those benighted lands; and sing in commemoration of what has taken place, (with a slight change in the lines,) what was then sung in anticipation of these blessed events.

Hail! Isles of the South! your redemption proclaim;
   No more you repose in the borders of gloom;
The "Ancient of Days" has announc'd his glad name,
   And glory has dawn'd on the verge of the tomb.

The billows that girt ye, the wild wave that roam,
   The zephyrs that play where the ocean-storms cease,
Have borne the rich freight to your desolate shore,
   Convey'd the glad tidings of pardon and peace.

On the islands that sat in the regions of night,
   The lands of despair, to oblivion a prey,
The morning had open'd with healing and light,
   The young Star of Bethlehem has brought in the day.

The altar and idol in dust overthrown,
   The incense forbade that was hallow'd with blood,
The priest of Melchizedeck there does atone,
   And the shrines of Atooi are sacred to God.

And thou, Obookiah! now sainted above,
   Hast joy'd as the herald their missions disclose,
And the prayer has been heard, that the land thou didst love
   Might blossom as Sharon, and bud as the rose.

EPILOGUE

"Oh! How I want to see Hawai`i! But I think I never shall. God will do right -He knows what is best." ~ Henry `Opukaha`ia, 1818

"He wants to come home."

Deborah Li`ikapeka Lee heard these five simple words in the early-morning hours of October 11, 1992. Although she was living in Washington State at the time, Lee was convinced it was God's voice calling her to bring back the body of her family member, Henry `Opukaha`ia (Obookiah), to Hawai`i. He was the very first fruit of the Hawaiian people to accept Jesus Christ as his Savior in the early 1800s while living with a Christian family in Connecticut. He was learning the Bible at Yale College, but died from sickness before returning to his beloved island home to tell others about Christianity. For 175 years his body rested in a country graveyard in Cornwall, Connecticut.

Though his physical body betrayed him, `Opukaha`ia's spirit flourished during his final days. His faith knew no bounds as he continually learned more of God's word and promises. Finally, when death was near, he made one startling request, and then a bold declaration, to those gathered around. First, he asked others to bring the good news of Jesus Christ to the Hawaiian people in order to free them from their present way of life and pagan religion. The second was leaving the fate of his earthly remains securely in God's hands. "Oh! How I want to see Hawai`i! But I think I never shall," Henry raised his arms and spoke through a flood of tears. "God will do right -He knows what is best."

`Opukaha`ia's request for missionaries to go to his homeland was quickly fulfilled by many Christian believers living in the New England area. Bolstered by his outstanding faith, they willingly left the comfort of their homes and took the gospel message with them. They made the almost year-long journey over tumultuous seas and arrived in the Hawaiian Islands, where many thousands of lost souls eventually came to a true and saving faith.

`Opukaha`ia's confidence that God would do what was right concerning his earthly body seemed misplaced. Over the years, many other people had attempted to bring his remains back home to Hawai`i, but all had failed. However, Lee, his first cousin, seven times removed, was certain she was a part of the Lord's gracious plan to bring `Opukaha`ia back to his final resting place on the hillside at the grounds of Kahikolu Church overlooking Kealakekua Bay on the Big Island. Although she was warned it might take 10 years or more to achieve her goal, Lee remained steadfast and dedicated to God's calling.

Not only was the effort time consuming, it was costly to make `Opukaha`ia's dream a reality. A group of his ohana and close family friends gathered as "Ahahui O `Opukaha`ia" to spearhead the effort. Individual citizens, community members, schools, and businesses also supported the project.

God had also placed key people in the right place at exactly the needed time. Deborah's parents, Kwai Wah and Elizabeth Lee, along with Uncle Billy Paris Jr. of Kainaliu became integral people involved in moving the homecoming forward. The Rev. David Hirano, and the Rev. Carmen Wooster, who resided in Hartford, graciously volunteered to complete the needed leg work on the mainland. The Rev. Tom Walter, a minister of the gospel in Connecticut at the time, and a blood relative of Opukaha'ia, met with people in the community of Cornwall about the importance of bringing his body back to the islands. The effort was also assisted by a United States Congressional Repatriation Act that effectively removed all legal obstacles from Lee to claim her fallen family member. Miraculously, it only took 10 months, from start to finish, as God opened door after door for `Opukaha`ia's safe return. "It was the Lord's doing, to show how magnificent and powerful He is," Lee said.

When it came time to unearth `Opukaha`ia's body, it was an answer to prayer as archeologists found his skeletal remains, known as "'Iwi" in the Hawaiian language, still intact. His body was removed from its 175-year resting place and was respectfully placed in a beautiful koa casket. Once secure, it was brought to the United Church of Christ in Cornwall, Connecticut, where a large congregation had gathered at his farewell worship service. The casket was then flown to Honolulu, where he was honored by many generations of Christians blessed to know true faith in Jesus Christ because of his original heartfelt plea. A special service of praise, worship, and remembrance was held at the Hawaii Conference United Church of Christ's Boardroom on behalf of the Woman's Board of Missions for the Pacific Islands, the organization that owns the copyright to his memoirs. The Rev. Edith Wolfe, a former executive director of the mission organization, attended the service. She was responsible for bringing the knowledge of Henry `Opukaha`ia's legacy back to Hawaii. Rev.Wolfe had also written the forward and served as the editor for the 1968 printed edition of this book.

Three more special services followed on Oahu at Kawaiaha`o Church, Kamehameha School's Kapalama Campus, and, finally, Kaumakapili Church.

`Opukaha`ia's body was flown to the Big Island on August 6, 1993 and was greeted in a Hawaiian-style homecoming. His casket was driven to Honaunau Bay, in the City of Refuge, where it was honored and blessed before it was placed between two canoes that were bound together. The Keoua Canoe Club gently paddled his body towards Kealakekua Bay, the exact location where `Opukaha`ia had jumped into the ocean to escape the violence of constant tribal feuding, and the darkness of his heathen culture. The skies had been ominous, heavy, and gloomy all day, as if mourning the loss of a native son. As the canoe made the turn into the bay, however, the sun broke free of the clouds, bursting forth in all its glory, casting an unforgettable radiant light on the processional. It was as if the doorway at the hinge of eternity had swung wide open and God, Himself, was saying, "Well done, my good and faithful servant. Welcome home." As if on cue, the dolphins began to jump and spin around the canoe. With maile lei wrapped around his neck, `Opukaha`ia's relative and namesake, Henry Keau Kamoha`ula `Opukaha`ia Kelii Hoomanawanui seemed to possess his cousin's spirit as he jumped from the vessel and swam to shore to make the final journey safely back to shore. The red glow of the blazing sun framed Kamoha`ula perfectly, but the second he touched the rocks, it immediately withdrew and faded back into the clouds. The canoe continued towards the wharf, where the crowd sang "Nu Oli" and offered up prayers of thanksgiving to the true and living God for bringing Henry `Opukaha`ia home to Hawai'i. The throng of people then followed the awaiting hearse containing `Opukaha`ia's remains up the steep pali to attend an evening praise and worship service at Kahikolu (Trinity) Congregational Church in Kepulu, South Kona.

Over the course of the next week, `Opukaha`ia's earthly remains were taken to the four corners of the island. He was first honored at the Henry `Opukaha`ia Memorial Chapel in Punalu'u, followed by a luau lunch at Kauaha`ao Congregational Church. He was then taken to Haili Congregational Church in Hilo, the site of the great awakening of faith in Hawaii and eventually spread the gospel throughout the Pacific Rim. The final leg of his long journey brought his remains to Kailua-Kona for services at Mokuaikaua Church, the oldest church on the Big Island, and then to the University of the Nations. From there, the casket made its way up the hill to Lanakila Church in Kainaliu before reaching its blessed resting place on Sunday, August 15, 1993, at the Kahikolu (Trinity) Congregational Church Cemetery. `Opukaha`ia had finally come full circle, to the place where his journey into eternal life had begun. Lee knew it was a divine appointment by the Creator of the universe and she would never forget the tender mercies allowed to fulfill the obligation to her ancestor. "It showed the Lord is living and breathing and here," she said "It is in God's time, not our time," she said. "Henry got the best of the best. The Lord had his hand in everything, everything, everything. It was a wonderful tribute to Henry."

Henry`Opukaha`ia's life and legacy are far from over. He continues to live in the hearts and minds of countless people in Hawai`i, and throughout the world. Although Henry `Opukaha`ia was lost to the earthly world the day he passed away, he was never lost to God, nor was his impact on mankind forgotten. His name, enduring faith, and his ultimate place in history are perpetuated in righteousness and will forever be remembered. He will continue to be loved, cherished, and honored whenever his story is told. The third Sunday in February will always be celebrated as `Opukaha`ia Sunday at Kahikolu and other churches throughout the Hawaiian Islands and beyond.

Respectfully Submitted,
Karen Welsh, President
Woman's Board of Missions for the Pacific Islands
Big Island Representative
January 30, 2012

PUBLICATION INFORMATION

THE FIRST EDITION of the Memoirs of Henry Obookiah was published at the offices of the Religious Intelligencer in New Haven in 1818, a few months after Obookiah's death. A second printing bears the date 1819. The first two editions were copyrighted to Lyman Beecher and Joseph Harvey, and included the full text of Beecher's Funeral Oration and Harvey's Inaugural Sermon at the installation of the Rev. Herman Daggett as principal of the Foreign Mission School in 1817. The Rev. Harvey was the Congregational minister at neighboring Goshen. A Sunday School edition printed in 1830 has Owhyhee, no chapter headings, and an excerpt from Beecher's funeral oration. The American Tract Society printed two editions both with no dates, but The National Union Catalogue lists one as published in 1831 and the other in 1847. Both editions are divided into chapters, have a Table of Contents, use the word Hawaii instead of Owhyhee and have added a chapter entitled "Conclusion". The American Tract Society underwrote an 1867 edition in the Hawaiian language. The Hawaiian translation included additional information obtained by the translator Rev. S. W. Papaula, a minister at Kealakekua, Hawai'i from people who remembered Opukaha'ia and his family. Other translations of the Memoirs include one in language of the Choctaw Indians and another in the Maltese (Greek).

THIS EDITION, while retaining the 1818 title page with some exceptions, includes many of the changes incorporated in the later Revised Editions by the American Tract Society. The Table of Contents, chapter divisions and headings, and the "Conclusion" section come from these editions. Opukaha'ia, his Hawaiian name, has been used when referring to him in the Hawaiian context. Henry Obookiah is used with the New England notes and photographs.

THE ROUTE BACK TO HAWAII FROM CORNWALL, CONNECTICUT FOR HENRY OPUKAHA'IA'S REMAINS

Dated: July 9, 1993

I.   Sunday, July 25, 1993: Cornwall, Connecticut A Farewell Service, 2:30 p.m. at the United Church of Christ in Cornwall (8 Bolton Hill Rd).

II.   Monday, July 26, 1993: Depart from Hartford, Connecticut to Hawaii.

III.   Wednesday, July 28, 1993: Public Respect to Henry, 9:00 am. to 4:00 p.m., Hawaii Conference, United Church of Christ (15 Craigside Place, Nuuanu Avenue).

IV.   Sunday, August 1, 1993: Kawaiahao Church, 2:00 p.m.

V.   Tuesday & Wednesday, August 3-4, 1993: Public Respect to Henry, 7:30 a.m. to 4:00 p.m., Bishop Memorial Chapel, (Kamehameha Schools Campus).

VI.   Thursday, August 5, 1993: Kaumakapili Church, Evening Service, 7:30 p.m.

VII.   Friday, August 6, 1993: Arrival at Keahole Airport
1. To Honaunau; by canoe to Kealakekua Bay (Keoua Canoe Club)
2. Welcome Home ceremonies, 5:00 p.m., Kealakekua Bay
3. Evening Service, 7:00 p.m., Kahikolu Congregational Church

VIII.   Saturday, August 7, 1993: Morning Service, 10:00 a.m. Henry Opukaha'ia Memorial Chapel, Punalu'u, Ka'u (The luau to follow, Kauaha'o Congregational Church Hall, Waiohinu)

IX.   Sunday & Monday, August 8-9, 1993: Haili Congregational
         Sunday: Public Respect to Henry, 4:00 to 6:00 p.m.; Memorial
         Service, 6:00 to 7:00 p.m.
         Monday: Public Respect to Henry, 1:00 to 5:00 p.m.; Aha Mele,
         7:00 p.m.

X.   Wednesday, August 11, 1993: Mokuaikaua Church, 6:00 p.m.
         Service.

XI.   Thursday & Friday, August 12-13, 1993: Public Respect to
         Henry, 8:00 a.m.(Lanakila Congregational Church).

XII.   Saturday, August 14, 1993: Public Respect to Henry, 8:00 a.m.
         (Kahikolu Congregational Church).

XIII.   Sunday, August 15, 1993:   Concluding Program, 3:00 p.m.; The
         Interment of Henry Opukaha'ia (Kahikolu Congregational
         Church Cemetery, Napo'opo'o, Kona). The Welcome Home
         Luau, 5:00 p.m.

GRAVE SITE DESCRIPTION

The tomb is located on the property of Kahikolu Church, on the cliffs of Kealakekua Bay, where Henry `Opukaha`ia first jumped off the rocks and into the water to run away on the sailing vessel. (Karen Welsh Photos)

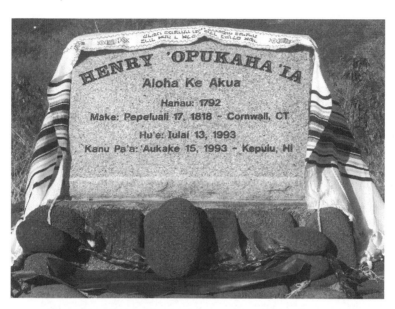

Deborah Li'ikapeka Lee at the tomb of her cousin Henry, located at Kahikolu Church on the Big Island of Hawaii.

NOTES

THE TITLE PAGE: This form of the Title Page is taken from the 1818 and 1819 editions of the *Memoirs of Henry Obookiah;* exceptions will be noted.

"Memoirs": The original title of this book, when it appeared in 1818 was *Memoirs of Henry Obookiah.* In later editions the word was changed to *"Memoir".* We use "Memoirs" because that is the original title.

"Henry Obookiah": This was the name he was known by in New England. "Henry" was a name given the young man by American sailors who could not pronounce his Hawaiian name. Henry explains the custom himself, saying: "...my fellow-traveller, by name Thomas Hopoo—Thomas, a name given him by the supercargo of the ship." His Hawaiian name, *Opukaha'ia,* was spelled phonetically by the New Englanders who taught the Hawaiian youth to read and write. His signature on a letter to Mrs. Florilla M. Ripley verifies his spelling of the name. (See Photo section) The Hawaiian name, *Opukaha'ia,* literally means "Stomach-slashed-open." According to Hawaiian historian, Charles W. Kenn, it commemorated "an event in which a chief was disemboweled."

"A Native of Owhyhee": Owhyhee is derived from the phonetic spelling of Hawai'i first used by Captain James Cook in December 1778 as he wrote in his journal, "In the evening we discovered another island to windward which the natives call *O'why'he."* Owhyhee remained the spelling until the American missionaries decided upon the orthography of the Hawaiian language. The first edition of the Hawaiian alphabet printed on the Mission Press, January 7, 1822, uses the abbreviation *Owhy.,* but the second printing in September 1822 has *Hawaii.*

"A Member of the Foreign Mission School": The school was established under auspices of the American Board of Commissioners for Foreign Missions, on October 29, 1816, when the Constitution was adopted at a meeting at the home of the Rev. Dr. Timothy Dwight in New Haven. Article 2 of the Constitution of the school stated: "The object of this school shall be the education of the heathen youth in such a manner, as

that with future professional studies, they may be qualified to become useful missionaries, schoolmasters, interpreters, physicians, or surgeons, among heathen nations, and to communicate such information in agriculture and the arts, as shall tend to Christianity and civilization."

Classes began in 1817 in the town of Cornwall, Connecticut, with Edwin W. Dwight in charge. The School continued until 1826. Missionaries Dr. Thomas Holman, Elisha Loomis, and Samuel Ruggles; Dexter and Nathan Chamberlain, sons of Captain Daniel Chamberlain; and the Hawaiian youths, Thomas Hopu, William Kanui, John Honoli'i, and George Kaumuali'i, all attended the Foreign Mission School prior to their departure for Hawai'i on the Brig *Thaddeus* with the Sandwich Isles Mission, October 23, 1819.

"Who Died at Cornwall, Connecticut, February 17, 1818, aged 26 years." The death of the young Hawaiian had been anticipated as word of his illness spread to neighboring villages. The Rev. Dr. Lyman Beecher preached a lengthy sermon at the meeting house; and Edwin W. Dwight spoke at the graveside. The age recorded on Obookiah's tombstone is probably as close as any of his contemporaries could determine and indicated a birthdate of 1792. If this date was correct Obookiah would have been sixteen when he left Hawaii in 1808. The Rev. S. W. Papaula changed the birthdate to 1787 in the Hawaiian edition of the *Memoirs* in 1867, after talking with elderly Hawaiians in the Kealakekua Bay area of Hawai'i.

"By Edwin W. Dwight": The first editions of the *Memoirs of Henry Obookiah* gave no author's name, but later editions listed "The Rev. E. W. Dwight, First Instructor of the "Foreign Mission School" as the author. Edwin Welles Dwight, a native of Stockbridge, Massachusetts, had completed three years at Williams College before he transferred to Yale College to enroll in its Divinity School. He befriended a weeping Obookiah sitting on the steps of Yale, instructed him and placed him in the household of his kinsman, the Rev. Dr. Timothy Dwight, President of Yale. Dwight was in Litchfield, Connecticut, studying for the ministry under the Rev. Dr. Lyman Beecher when he was asked to take charge of "Owhyhee boys at the Heathen School" in April 1817. Dwight later was minister of a Congregational Church in Richmond, Massachusetts.

CHAPTER I

"Hawaii, the most important…:" The center of the population and power was on the island of Hawai'i with a resident population in the early 1800's of about 85,000, from a total population estimated at 130,000 to 150,000 for the entire island chain according to William Ellis in *Polynesian Researches.* The center of population in the Hawaiian Islands shifted to O'ahu after the death of Kamehameha I, when the Hawaiian monarchy took up residence in Honolulu on the island of O'ahu.

"The Sandwich Islands" were discovered by the famous English explorer Captain James Cook in 1778 and named for his patron, the Earl of Sandwich, First Lord of the Admiralty. This name remained in popular use until the 1840 Constitution substituted the name *Hawaiian Islands* for *Sandwich Islands* in its Preamble.

Obookiah's birthdate: "…about the year 1792. The birthdate listed in the *Memoirs* was only an approximate date decided upon by his New England friends. Hawaiian sources say Opukaha'ia was born in 1787 in Ka'u at Ninole, on the island of Hawai'i. This would have made him twenty-one when he left Hawai'i.

Mother's name: In the 1867 Hawaiian edition, the Rev. S. W. Papaula states that Opukaha'ia's mother's name was *Kamahoula.*

Father's name: Opukaha'ia's father's name is given as *Keau* in the Hawaiian edition.

"…in a war made after the old king died…" In a translation of the 1867 Hawaiian edition by Charles W. Kenn, it is stated that Opukaha'ia's parents were killed during the war between Kamehameha I and Namakeha in the battle of Kaipalaoa. The year was 1797, when Opukaha'ia was ten years old.

A Narrative of Five Youths from the Sandwich Islands is a pamphlet which was "Published By Order of the Agents Appointed to Establish a School for the Heathen Youth" in 1816. The sub-title reads: "Viz: Obookiah, Hopoo, Tennooe, Honooree, and Prince Tamoree Now

Receiving An Education in This Country." It contained descriptions of the lives and prospects of Henry Obookiah (Opukaha'ia), Thomas Hopoo (Hopu), William Tennooe (Kanui), John Honoree (Honoli'i), and George Tamoree (Kaumuali'i). The pamphlet was sold to promote involvement and funds from the Christian public to support the Foreign Mission School.

"Captain Brintnall, master…": Captain Caleb Brintnall, master of the *Triumph* out of New Haven, Connecticut, befriended Obookiah and Hopoo while anchored at Kealakekua Bay,
Hawai'i. When the ship was sold in New York, Brintnall invited the two Hawaiian youths to accompany him to his home in New Haven. Captain Brintnall was one of the owners of the vessel as well as the master.

"…my fellow-traveler, by name Thomas Hopoo…"   Obookiah's companion on the voyage to New England remained his staunch friend for the remainder of his life. Thomas Hopu returned to Hawai'i with the Sandwich Islands Mission to assist the New Englanders in the conversion of the Hawaiian people. He was a participant in the first Christian marriage among Hawaiians, but grew discouraged as the Mission denied him a license to preach the Gospel.

"…by name Russel Hubbard, …": Russell Hubbard, the eldest son of General John Hubbard, is said to have studied for the ministry after graduation from Yale College, but a love of travel drove him abroad. His voyage on the *Triumph* was his last as he was lost at sea in November or December, 1810, on a passage from New Haven to the West Indies. He was 27 years old.

CHAPTER II

"We landed in New York in 1809." The name of the ship is not mentioned in the *Memoirs*, but the *Connecticut Herald* of Tuesday, August 8, 1809. Volume VI. No. 302, carried the following notice:
"The ship *Triumph* (Captain Caleb) Brintnall, belonging to this port, has arrived at New York in 5 months from Canton. The *Triumph* sailed

from New Haven the 9th of January, 1807, on a sealing voyage to the Pacific Ocean and China…"

"How strange to see females eat with men." Women were not allowed to eat with men in ancient Hawai'i. This *kapu* was broken after the death of Kamehameha I when the Queen Regent Ka'ahumanu and Kamehameha's young son, Liholiho, sat down to eat together, signaling the end of the *kapu* system.

"In this place [New Haven] I became acquainted with many students belonging to the college." Yale College was founded in 1701 to assure an educated clergy for New England churches.

"…Mr. E. W. Dwight, who first taught me to read and write." Edwin Welles Dwight, the divinity student who first encountered Obookiah at Yale, was the author of the *Memoirs*. Dwight was very modest and always refers to himself as "his early friend."

"…the letter R—a letter which occasioned him more trouble than all the others. In pronouncing it, he uniformly gave it the sound of L." The American missionaries had difficulty deciding between using the R and L when they set up the Hawaiian alphabet. Before the orthography was settled, the R and L were used interchangably. Early maps show "Honoruru", "Kairua" and "Hiro", instead of Honolulu, Kailua and Hilo.

"He then wished me to live with President Dwight." The Rev. Dr. Timothy Dwight, president of Yale College, was one of the Agents of the American Board of Commissioners for Foreign Missions to set up the Constitution for the founding of the Foreign Mission School at Cornwall, Connecticut, in 1816. President Dwight and student Edwin W. Dwight were distantly related.

"Samuel J. Mills" was Samuel John Mills, Jr., one of the young undergraduate students at Williams College in Williamstown, Massachusetts, who dedicated himself to service in the foreign mission field at the famous "Haystack Prayer Meeting" in 1806. Out of their prayers arose the American Board of Commissioners for Foreign Missions. Young Mills wrote the following to his friend Gordon Hill after meeting Obookiah at Yale in 1809: "I propose to leave town in two weeks with this native of the South to accompany me to

Torringford, ...Here I intend he shall stay until next spring......Thus, you see, he is likely to be fairly fixed by my side."

"Torringford, Connecticut" is a small town in the Litchfield hills in western Connecticut. Litchfield County was a center of evangelical religious thought in the early part of the 19th century.

"I say what is the chief end of man," Obookiah was evidently learning the Westminster Catechism whose first question asks: "What is the chief end of man?" The answer: "To glorify God and to enjoy Him forever." The Westminster Catechism, dating from the seventeenth century, was widely used by both Congregational and Presbyterian churches.

CHAPTER III

"I left Torringford and went to Andover."   Andover, Massachusetts, a town about twenty miles northwest of Boston, was the site of Andover Theological Seminary, founded in 1808 by the Congregationalists.

"...I boarded at the house of Deacon Hasseltine, the family of Mrs. Judson, Missionary to Burmah..." Rev. and Mrs. Adoniram Judson were the first missionaries sent out by the American Board of Commissioners

for Foreign Missions in 1812. It was a blow to the Congregational mission movement when word was received in January 1813, that the Judsons had become Baptists en route to India and had severed their ties with the ABCFM.

A fellow boarder at Deacon Jno. Hasseltine's house, Joshua Coffin, remembered Obookiah in a March 1859 letter: "In the summer of 1811 I attended the Academy in Bradford, and was a boarder in the family of Deacon Jno. Hasseltine, whose family then consisted of himself, his wife, son, three daughters Abigail, Mary, Ann, afterwards Mrs. Judson and several boarders, among whom was that very interesting native of Ohwyhee, Obookiah. frankness, honesty and simplicity that no one could be offended with him....He afterwards as you know became a very devout Christian."

"I went to Tyngsbury last week to see a boy who came from Hawaii." Tyngsborough, Massachusetts, is a small town about twelve miles from Andover.

"Obookiah went to spend several months at Hollis, New Hampshire." Hollis is just over the New Hampshire line not too far from Tyngsbury, Massachusetts. The church, founded in 1743, is still in existence although the building which was there in Obookiah's day burned in 1923.

"Deacon E." Well-preserved records of the Hollis Church tell us that this was Deacon Daniel Emerson, Jr., son of the Rev. Daniel Emerson, first pastor of the church.

"Deacon B." was Deacon Ephraim Burge.

"Rev. Mr. S." was Rev. Eli Smith, pastor of the Hollis Church, 1793-1831.

"Doctor C." was Doctor Benoni Cutter who settled in Hollis as a physician in 1799. He was greatly respected, both as a citizen and a physician. In the year 1814, he was appointed to the office of Deacon of the Hollis Church. He died on January 17, 1816.

CHAPTER IV

"...James Morris, Esq. of Litchfield,...." was the principal of the same academy that Samuel J. Mills, Jr., attended as a boy. Morris was also an Agent of the Foreign Mission School.

"At the Annual Meeting of the North Consociation of Litchfield County, in the fall of 1814, Henry....applied to that body to take him under their care...." "Under Care" is an official status in the Congregational churches, indicating that the person has made formal declaration of his intention to prepare himself to serve as a minister. The record of the meeting of the North Consociation on October 11, 1814, shows that the request was granted and that "Reverend Messrs. Samuel J. Mills, Joseph Harvey

and Dea. Saml Norton be a committee to have the oversight of Henry's affairs and advise him respecting his studies...."

At the next Annual Meeting of the Consociation, September 26, 1815, this is recorded:

The trustees of Henry Obookiah made report which was accepted, whereupon it was Voted that the 28 dollars now remaining in the hands of Mr. Harvey be given to him as a compensation for the board of Henry Obookiah till last spring. And that the same patronage be extended to Thomas Hoopoo and William Tennooe, his countrymen, so far as to provide a place for their board and schooling for one year." *(The original minutes of the Litchfield north Consociation from 1792 to 1881 are in the Archives Room of the Congregational House, Hartford, Connecticut.)*

"....the Rev. Mr. Harvey of Goshen." The Rev. Joseph Harvey was the minister at Goshen, Connecticut, a few miles from Cornwall, and was one of the seven Agents of the American Board charged with setting up the Foreign Mission School. His inauguration sermon is bound into the early editions of the *Memoirs.*

CHAPTER V

"I want to see you about our Grammar." See photo section for Page One of the Hawaiian Grammar prepared by Obookiah, evidently with the help of the Rev. Eleazar T. Fitch of New Haven. A note in early editions of the *Memoirs* reads: "....Obookiah received the assistance of the Rev. Mr. F. now Professor of Divinity for Yale College." This was the Rev. Eleazar Thompson Fitch, D.D., professor of Sacred Literature at Yale 1822-24, and from 1824 until his retirement in 1852, the Livingston Professor of Divinity and Lecturer in Homiletics. Professor Fitch was a linguist who taught Greek in his early years at Yale.

"I have been translating a few chapters of the Bible into the Hawaiian language." Later in the *Memoirs* the author tells us that Obookiah translated the book of Genesis into Hawaiian. There is no other record of other chapters also being translated at that time. The manuscript of the Hawaiian translation of Genesis has not been found.

"….the Rev. Mr. Prentice of Canaan." The Rev. Charles Prentice was one of the seven Agents of the American Board charged with setting up the Foreign Mission School.

"I was visited this morning by a pious and good Rev. Mr. H. of L." This may refer to Rev. Dr. Hyde of Lee, Massachusetts, not far from Canaan, Connecticut.

"The devoted Brainerd;" The Rev. David Brainerd, missionary to the American Indians, died at age twenty-nine. His autobiography, showing a deep and sensitive Christian spirit of dedication, influenced many young people to serve the missionary cause.

CHAPTER VI

"Mr. Ephraim Burge, Jun. of the State of New York." This was the son of the Deacon Ephraim Burge in whose home Obookiah had lived while he was in Hollis, New Hampshire.

The trip with Mr. Perkins for the Board of Commissioners for Foreign Missions was undertaken to promote interest in and funds for the Foreign Mission School.

From the Records of the Prudential Committee for November 5, 1816:

"As several of the gentlemen appointed within a year past for the purpose of promoting the funds of the Board have found it inconvenient to fulfil their appointments: therefore RESOLVED that the Rev. Nathan Perkins of Amherst, Rev. Charles Prentice of Canaan *(and several others including Samuel Mills and Joseph Harvey)* be commissioned as agents for promoting the funds of the Board generally & for the education of heathen youth particularly.

Mr. Perkins reported on the success of his trip, on which Obookiah had accompanied him:

Amherst, Jan. 21, 1817—

Rev. Sir,

I duly rec'd yours appointing me as an Agent to solicit contributions, and to form Charitable Societies, "within convenient limits," for the Education of Heathen Youth in our Country. Previous to receiving, and without expecting this appointment, I had sent to the Committee of the Heathen School in Connecticut, for *Henry Obookiah*, that with him I might visit a few adjacent Towns, which had been blessed with the effusions of the Spirit, in order to obtain contributions for the Education of him and his associates. He did not, however, arrive at my house, until after I had received my Commission from the Prudential Committee. He *then* came, with permission to stay with me four or five week; or, as the letter of James Morris, Esq. expressed it, "a longer time if I judged it necessary." With reference to what I have (al)ready done, and to the effects produced on the minds of the Community, in consequence of having Henry with me in the Towns I visited, I request a further indulgence from the Committee that he may continue with me, several weeks longer. To this request I can think of no objection, except that it will hinder him in the prosecution of his Studies. But this objection lost part of its force, by the fact that he has the privilege of studing with me, every day of leisure he enjoys, and I apprehend it is wholly removed when we consider the objects gained by his being with me. These objects, are, a liberal contribution, and an awakening in the Christian public, a Foreign Missionary spirit. That these objects have been gained is evident from actual experiment. It is truly astonishing to see what effects are produced on the feelings of the people by seeing Henry, and hearing him converse. It opens the hearts and hands even of enemies. Many have contributed generously who never contributed before. If pecuniary excess attends my exertion in future, as it has during the past, the funds of the Heathen School will be increased from 1000 to 1200 or perhaps 1500 Dollars. But the most pleasing effect is, that it rouses a Foreign Missionary Spirit. Yes, Sir, I trust that in the Towns I have already visited, this Spirit is awakened to sleep no more. This effect I had not anticipated. Surely it is an object worth gaining; and if it can be accomplished by a few weeks of Henry's time, may not that be sacrificed? I shall write soon on this same subject to the Comm. of the School. I am yours, etc.

N. Perkins, Jr.

CHAPTER VII

"….the parting salutation of his native language, 'Alloah o e'." "Aloha 'Oe" can mean "Farewell to thee" as in the famous song written much by late Queen Lili'oukalani or, as it is translated here, "My love be with you."

"Conclusion" was added to the *Memoir* approximately 13 years after the death of Henry Obookiah when the American Tract Society published the revised edition. The statement that "twenty-four missionaries and forty-two assistants" were laboring in Obookiah's homeland when this edition was published points to the 1831 date. By 1831 four companies of missionaries had landed in the Hawaiian Islands with twenty-four male missionaries and forty-two females and native helpers. Lahainaluna High School was founded in 1831 to educate "native teachers and preachers."

"Kaahumanu" (Ka'ahumanu) was the favorite wife of Kamehameha I and *kuhina nui* (co-ruler) with his son Liholiho after his death. Baptized on December 5, 1825, she took the Christian name of Elizabeth.

Keopualini (Keopuolani), the sacred wife of Kamehameha I, was baptized as she lay dying. When her death came on September 17, 1823, her funeral was conducted with the solemnity and Christian ceremonies she had requested.

INDEX

ABOUT THE WOMAN'S BOARD OF MISSIONS FOR THE PACIFIC ISLANDS

The Woman's Board of Missions for the Pacific Islands is a group of compassionate Christian women who come from a variety of churches and diverse backgrounds to reach out in many practical ways to those in need, especially women and children, providing financial support both in Hawai'i and abroad. The ministry of our organization was founded in 1871 and is affiliated with the United Church of Christ.

Governed by an unwavering faith and core values of competence, compassion, character, and community, our purpose is to inspire and empower women to become active Christians, nurturing the Spirit in their individual lives, homes, community and the entire world, to educate and encourage children in their highest potential, and to be in partnership with sister organizations sharing similar values.

The Woman's Board of Missions for the Pacific Islands has supported numerous projects and organizations that include but are not limited to the UCCP Pasuquin Learning Center, a preschool in the Philippines, the UCC Transition House, a safe house for women and their children who are survivors of Domestic Violence, the Women's Community Correctional Center in Hawai'i, ZOE International, an organization that rescues children from human trafficking, and the Waikiki Youth Outreach Center, an outreach service providing hot meals, clothing, medical care, and basic necessities for our homeless youth.

Additionally, our organization grants annual gifts to women who attend seminary through the Mother Alice Fund, gifts for mission endeavors in Micronesia, through the Micronesia Missionary Memorial Fund, one-time financial gifts to meet a special need of individuals or families through The Family Thank Offering, and scholarships for women and children throughout the Pacific through the Edith H. Wolfe Fund.

As the needs of our communities and world continue to increase exponentially, more resources and willing servants are required to help meet these needs. Today, you can greatly help to further the ministry of the Woman's Board of Missions for the Pacific Islands with a financial gift and/or a commitment to serve. Monetary gifts can be sent to the address below. Membership applications and more information about us are available on our website at http://hcucc.org/?page_id=2526. You are also invited to like us on Facebook at https://w.facebook.com/pages/Womans-Board-of-Missions-For-The-Pacific-Islands/171074089640951.

Woman's Board of Missions for the Pacific Islands
1848 Nuuanu Avenue
Honolulu, Hawai'i 96817
(808) 791-5647

ABOUT WRITER KAREN WELSH

She is passionate about serving as the current president of the Woman's Board of Missions for the Pacific Islands and enjoys ministry at Haili Congregational Church in Hilo, where her husband, Brian, serves as Kahu (Pastor). She is blessed beyond measure that her own grandchildren, Noah Ikaika and Alexa Nohea, are descendants of Henry Opukaha'ia's lineage.

Professionally, she is a freelance writer and photographer and invites you to visit her website at www.karenwelsh.com.

Made in the USA
Charleston, SC
06 October 2012